DISCARD

PHILOSOPHY OF RELIGION SERIES

Editor's Note

The philosophy of religion is one of several very active branches of philosophy today, and the present series is designed both to consolidate the gains of the past and to direct attention upon the problems of the future. Between them these volumes will cover every aspect of the subject, introducing it to the reader in the state in which it is today, including its open ends and growing points. Thus the series is designed to be used as a comprehensive textbook for students. But it is also offered as a contribution to present-day discussion; and each author will accordingly go beyond the scope of an introduction to formulate his own position in the light of contemporary debates.

JOHN HICK

Philosophy of Religion Series

General Editor: John Hick, H. G. Wood Professor of Theology,
University of Birmingham

John Hick (Birmingham University) *Arguments for the Existence of God*
H. P. Owen (King's College, London) *Concepts of Deity*
Kai Nielsen (Calgary University) *Contemporary Critiques of Religion*
Basil Mitchell (Oriel College, Oxford) *The Justification of Religious Belief*
William A. Christian (Yale University) *Oppositions of Religious Doctrines:*
A Study in the Logic of Dialogue among Religions
Ninian Smart (Lancaster University) *The Phenomenon of Religion*
M. J. Charlesworth (Melbourne University)
Philosophy of Religion: The Historic Approaches
Terence Penelhum (Calgary University) *Problems of Religious Knowledge*
H. D. Lewis (King's College, London) *The Self and Immortality*

THE PHENOMENON
OF RELIGION

NINIAN SMART

A Crossroad Book
THE SEABURY PRESS • NEW YORK

The Seabury Press
815 Second Avenue
New York, N.Y. 10017

Library of Congress Catalog Card Number: 72-8067
ISBN: 0-8164-1102-6

Printed in the United States of America

Contents

Introduction

If I may be permitted to be mildly autobiographical in this introduction, it is to be justified by the fact that it throws some light on the logic of what follows. When I was asked to contribute to the present series of books, basically in the philosophy of religion, and to write about the phenomenon of religion, I was naturally delighted and alarmed. Delighted because of the kindness shown to me by Professor John Hick in choosing me for this; but alarmed because the task presented a dilemma. To write adequately about the phenomenon (or phenomena) of religion would require an exhaustive survey of types of cults, beliefs, experiences, institutions, social arrangements, symbolisms, and so forth. This was both beyond the scope of a book of this size and beyond my knowledge and powers. On the other hand something in this direction ought to be performed, especially in a series devoted to the philosophy of religion. In writing the book I have tried to keep two strategies in mind: first, to concentrate somewhat on the methods required in the study of religion, for questions of method are inevitably of importance to the philosopher. Second, I have tried to present a certain amount of theory about religion which I hope is relevant to philosophy. These strategies can be illuminated a little by my becoming a bit autobiographical – not that my biography in itself is of any special interest to the reader, but because I have been fortunate in being able to be a *bricoleur*, as Lévi-Strauss might put it, of relevant experiences in the two fields of enquiry at issue, namely philosophy and religion. For the philosophy of religion inevitably both suffers and gains from its straddling of two worlds.

In the English-speaking world the philosophy of religion has been heavily influenced by the concerns of post-war analytic philosophy. These had their most influential expression, in regard to religion, in the famous 'New Essays in Philosophical Theology' edited by A. G. N. Flew and A. C. MacIntyre, which appeared in 1956. In brief and crudely, the two main aspects of this treatment of religion had to do with problems about religious language and meaning on the one hand, and with questions of the truth of religion, given a framework of empiricism, on the other. Even now, a survey of the journals about a decade and a half later demonstrates how strong a grip these concerns have taken upon the deliberations of philosophers of religion. I am far from decrying these concerns; they remain important. But when I had the good fortune to be plunged into the philosophical world in the late forties and early fifties at Oxford, I felt a certain unease. This was partly due to my having been enabled to study Chinese while in the army and to have been stationed for quite some time in Ceylon, so that I had become somewhat orientalised in my interests. What struck me forcibly, and what struck a chord too in my formidable supervisor for graduate work, the late J. L. Austin, was this: that as in embarking on the philosophy of science one ought to know a fair amount of science, so in doing the philosophy of religion one should know a fair amount of religion. I shall come to the ambiguities of this idea in a moment. However, it remained very obvious that the Achilles heel of so-called linguistic analysis of religious language lay in its lack of concern with context and plurality.

By context I refer to the actual milieu, including ritual, in which religious language is actually used. The trend was to take religious utterances simply as metaphysical claims. This was bad analysis, though powerful in presenting the empiricist challenge to the meaningfulness of religious claims. By plurality I refer to the variegated types of religious claims and languages – even within the ambit of the Christian tradition little attempt was made in philosophy of religion to identify the nature and particular commitments and sentiments of the 'believer' (a figure liable to appear unheralded in articles and books, like his opposite and equally obscure opponent 'the sceptic' or the 'unbeliever'). Even more seriously there was little concern for religions outside the Christian tradition, or for that matter

2

systems of belief such as Marxism which might betray some at least of the characteristics of religious faith. It was therefore very much my good fortune and concern to become involved in working, roughly within the linguistic–analytic tradition, towards bringing the comparative study of religion to bear on the philosophy of religion. To repeat the main point in a nutshell: how can we philosophise about something without knowing what it is really like?

However, interests can turn the other way. My interests in the study of religion for its own sake must always have been quite strong, seeing that when I decided to write a dissertation on the philosophy of religion at Oxford, most of my philosophical friends, in the rationalistic and empiricist temper of those days, thought I must be somewhat eccentric and even unbalanced. After having taught philosophy in Wales and Yale (where I had the eminent good fortune of being able to study Pali with Paul Tedesco, a great scholar whose intellect was undimmed despite the experiences in a Nazi concentration camp which weakened his body), I became much more involved in the history of religions, working with Professor H. D. Lewis, in the History and Philosophy of Religion at the University of London. To Professor Lewis and others I owe a great deal – it was among other things my first experience of working in a Faculty of Theology. A similar milieu I found in the University of Birmingham, with its excellent Department of Theology.

However, the philosophical bug gets a grip and makes one ask questions about what one is trying to do. The study of Theology, for instance, comes under scrutiny, especially in the circumstances of a secular university like Birmingham. The present book attempts among other things to draw out the implications of the distinction between the study of Religion and the study of Theology. It has special existential force for me, this quest; for it was not so long after I moved to the Department of Religious Studies at the University of Lancaster, built on essentially different principles from a Faculty or Department of Theology, that I was asked to write this book. It is a result of reflecting on the logic of studying religion for its own sake, which is an enterprise of vital importance

3

for one involved in shaping a new pattern of studies in this field.

Nevertheless an ambiguity remains, to which I referred a little earlier, for if it be conceded that to philosophise about religion it is necessary 'to know a fair amount of religion' (this was the phrase I used), it is still unclear what knowing a fair amount constitutes in this context. I am not here worried about the quantitative question (common sense must apply here, presumably, as to what a 'fair' amount is), but rather with the qualitative one. When my post at Lancaster was advertised it was declared to be open to someone of any faith or none, and this was an excellent and necessary principle for a truly secular university; but yet the columns of *The Times* were not free from correspondence on the absurdity of such an advertisement. Surely to know a fair amount of religion is to *have* a fair amount of it. Is not faith a kind of qualification in this field? The treatment in the present book of the nature of the *phenomenological* enquiry into religion is in part I hope an answer to this challenge. There is a great deal of confusion in this whole matter, partly arising, incidentally, from lack of attention to context and plurality. 'Teaching Christianity' – the phrase is already highly ambiguous: in one context faith *is* a credential but according to another meaning it is not. And consider 'faith', of which there are many sorts. Is it a good credential to be a Jehovah's Witness? I ask the question, not out of a sense of superiority to such Witnesses, but only to ask whether this sort of commitment is necessarily a good background to teaching and research. No-one would pretend that research, for instance, is the gateway to Paradise. Nevertheless, religion is sufficiently important in human existence to be properly understood, and the present book is meant to be a small contribution to thinking about this project.

The shape of the book has been dictated in part by the above questions. The first two chapters are basically concerned with methods and distinctions between different kinds of intellectual pursuits. The most important distinction is that between doing Religion (by which I mean the study of religion, just as history in one sense is the study of history in another) and doing (e.g., Christian) Theology. I have also tried to present an anatomy of the 'religious sciences'.

In the third Chapter I move to a consideration of the nature of myth, a heavily debated topic in recent times; and in the fourth to problems arising for religious belief out of the results of the scientific study of religion. I have not directly related these discussions, on the whole, to particular issues in current philosophy of religion, but I think their relevance is apparent. I shall try to indicate how in a moment. Before going on to this, however, I want to make clear a further point about my approach in this book.

I have attempted, within my powers, to be original in the treatment of topics. In this sense the book is not one kind of textbook. I have not attempted to expound other and well-known positions, though I may from time to time be indebted to them. For example, my account of myth obviously owes something to Otto and to Lévy-Bruhl (despite his being out of fashion); and my use of phenomenology would not have been possible without the work of van der Leeuw and others, however critical it may be necessary to be of them. I have tried to signpost affinities and debts. But I have deliberately eschewed the task of writing a critical history of the study of religion. First, others could do it better. Second, so many confusions, cultural accidents, personal quirks, lacks of knowledge, conceptual troubles, rationalisms and commitments have characterised the painful adolescence of the study of religion and religions that there is some advantage in writing about it as freely as possible. I am far from minimising the huge steps forward that have been made in the last century and in this, but I think it is fallacious to look on the development of a subject as being a matter of progressive consolidation. Hence my method of signposting both resemblances to the past and indebtednesses, rather than of beginning with the 'fathers' of the church of latter-day phenomenologists.

Now for the relevance of the treatment, with all its defects, to the philosophy of religion. First, the phenomenology of religion illuminates the necessity for the rather heavy contextualisation of religious utterances. For instance, some attention is paid here to the notion of the Focus of a rite (such as

Christ, in the case of the Eucharist). From this it is apparent that the existence or otherwise of Christ has to be treated experientially and in the context of ritual (e.g., worship). Similarly of course with God the Father and the God of the Muslims and so forth. This makes the task of analysing the existence claims a quite subtle one, bound to elude a straight verificationist model. Second, the attention paid in this book to a theory of myth bears a similar message, except that here I have tried to show that a proper treatment of myth involves the assumption of the numinosity of the divinities (or of some of them) appearing in the stories, which are themselves co-ordinated to ritual activities. This means that an important question for the philosophy of religion is the nature and 'validity' of the experience of the Holy (here of course I am somewhat indebted to Otto).

Third, I have attempted to describe the types of explanation which occur in Religion (that is, in the study of religion). Some of these necessarily impinge upon truth-claims in Theology, that is in the Expression of a given religion's claims. To this extent, I hope that the fourth Chapter, which is an essay on the possible tensions between religion and the science of religion, will be seen to be relevant to philosophical appraisals of religious truth-claims.

However, although I hope that the present enquiry will throw light on what now have become traditional problems in the philosophy of religion (since about the time of 'New Essays' or a bit earlier), I hope also that it will open a new perspective in philosophising: that is, I hope that questions of a philosophical nature arising in regard to the social sciences, as explored recently by a number of writers, will also be seen to have reference to the study of religion [1]. For in an important sense the study of religion is a social science, and an historical one. The phenomenology of religion, moreover, since it deals with so tricky and complex an area as religion – one which is also fogged by prejudice, idealism, insecurity, inspirations, naivetés, institutional pressures, ghastly rationalism, peculiar fideism, and so forth – has a great deal to contribute to other human enquiries in the attempt to reach an empathetic objectivity, or if you like a neutralist subjectivity. It is

6

in this a crucial part of the social and human sciences; for although it would be absurd to think that by understanding and describing a certain activity or point-of-view in all its richness you have *explained* it, it is surely a necessary first step before explanation. In other words, you have to know what the data are if you are explaining them. Human data, especially when directed at a transcendent Focus, are tricky. In brief, apart from the fact that attention to the phenomenology of religion may cast light on some 'traditional' philosophical problems about religion, it is important to see that the phenomenology of religion is a pursuit in its own right. As such its methods need philosophical scrutiny and will ultimately raise philosophical questions along their borderlines with other methods of enquiry.

Although I am very much committed to the broadening of the philosophy of religion so that it becomes the philosophy of religion and *religions* (thus escaping the secret identification of religion, in our Western culture, with the Judaeo-Christian tradition), I have largely drawn my examples from Christianity. Thus in the second essay (Chapter 2) I have attempted a phenomenological account of the Eucharist, while in the third I have made important use of the myth of Christ's life, death, and resurrection. This ploy has a double value: first, it treats of examples that are more likely to be familiar to the reader than many others that could have been used. Second, it deliberately treats Christianity in a phenomenological way, for in the past there has been too much of a sense that myths are what *other* men believe, too much of a sense that the comparative study of religion has to do with *non*-Christian religions. The frequent association of the philosophy of religion with Christian religion has itself militated against philosophising in a cool manner – stepping back from belief or anti-belief. My motto to that extent is not *Credo ut intelligam* (though I do not deny that this aphorism can be given an important phenomenological application); rather it is 'I understand in order that I may discuss'.

As I remarked earlier, in writing this book I have attempted within modest limits to be original and to express a particular line. To some extent my arguments rely on what I have written elsewhere. The disadvantage of having written quite a lot (for good or for ill) is that it goes against the grain to be too repetitive. For this reason I have peppered the notes with references to other writings of mine, as well of course to those of many others. This excess of self-reference is simply a consequence of previous polygraphy, combined with reluctance to churn out more of what went before. Naturally, some of what I regard as newer thoughts are the result of arguments and discussions with my students and colleagues, to whom I am most grateful.

1 Exploring Religion

In the whole firmament of intellectual values there is scarcely a more delightful, baffling, and profound pursuit than the exploration of religion. The study of religion, though it may still be in a trifle confused state, promises great advances. The basis of this hope lies in the conjunction of events which has brought us to the present fruitful intellectual and religious condition. Let me sketch these events briefly.

First, the nineteenth century sowed the seeds of a scientific study of religion [1]. The history of religions, the sociology of religion, anthropology, the psychology of religion – these are all essentially products of the nineteenth century. Naturally enough in that age of controversies some of the new theories, some of the applications of the historical method, were naive or twisted through apologetic or anti-religious motives. In a sharp form, men became aware of the reflexive character of the human sciences: to propound a theory about religion or to use historical methods to investigate the scriptures is to alter people's perception of their own tradition. Hence the heat which is often engendered. But the fires of those controversies have dwindled, partly through the reflexive assimilation of scientific studies into men's theologies, partly through a passing on to other concerns. Also, the diminution of religious authority among intellectuals has ineluctably brought about a relaxation of attitudes, a stronger possibility of 'distancing' oneself from one's own position, which facilitates the sympathetic yet objective exploration of religion (provided, that is, that the 'distance' is not too great).

This phenomenon is indeed an aspect of the second wave of events which join to form the basis of new confidence in the fruitfulness of the study of religion. The new situation of Christianity in more secularised environments, the ecumenical

9

movement, the interplay of world faiths in the post-colonial mood, the growing demands for mutual cultural respect, all these events add up to a spread of more pluralistic attitudes. Whether ultimately a sort of world religious pluralism is feasible or even to be commended, at the present juncture the mood is helpful for the sensitive study of religion.

Yet a demon may whisper: 'Doesn't the new mood itself signify a diminution of religion and a growing feeling that neither the issues nor hell burn any more? If so, then the study of religion may remain delightful and no doubt somewhat baffling, but it is no longer *important*.' Because he speaks for a large constituency, the demon is worth refuting with the following arguments, all of which in any case bear on some vital problems to be described in this book.

(i) The study of religion is not self-contained. The adequacy of Freud's psychology of religion bears upon his whole psychoanalytic scheme; the adequacy of Durkheim's account of the gods is highly relevant to the central issues of modern theoretical sociology; religious history illuminates (and is illuminated by) the rest of history.

(ii) It is partly a matter of convention as to what is counted under the head of religion and what is not. Can we know *a priori* that the methods of Weberian sociology will not work if applied to revolutionary China, just because Maoism is not regarded as religious [2]? Thus the study of religion is always liable to pass over into the study of movements which themselves challenge religious traditions, such as Marxism and atheism, and to explore a wider range of ideologies, even if they are not conventionally considered as theologies. This wider spread of the study of religion is typically obscured by institutional arrangements in higher education: the tradition of theology, as the mother of the study of religion, has created the sense that committed, religious people are licensed to study religion in a special Department or Faculty, while the study of atheism and ideologies belongs typically elsewhere. An irrational arrangement (alas, our 'subjects' here that we study are but confused, mixed shadows of the Forms laid up in the intellectual firmament).

10

(iii) The study of religion does not in the first instance determine the truth or otherwise of a faith or ideology. However, it is true, as I have said, that there is a reflexive relationship, and as knowledge of the explorations of religion become widely known, so men's perceptions of their traditions and their reasons for their belief or disbelief are altered. This dialectical relationship, to put it crudely, between the study of religion and theology is most important, and will engage quite a lot of attention in the present book. In one direction, it generates problems in the philosophy of religion – problems about the criteria of truth and about compatibilities of explanation. (For instance, does the psychology of religion compete at all with a theological account of conversion?) But it would be merely vulgar to judge *a priori* that the study of religion will erode religion's challenge or the truth of a Gospel. Furthermore, the vulgarity wears more than one horn, for rationalistic atheism might as equally well be threatened, if there is a threat, by the study of religion.

In brief, the study of religion is itself strategic to some of the human sciences; it also passes over into the study of 'nonreligious' ideologies, and it does not *prima facie* diminish the stature of what it studies. It would be unfortunate if confusion on these matters should inhibit the growth of the systematic study of religion, for this remains badly underdeveloped. This may seem, however, a paradoxical thing to say in view of the great resources, both in universities and in seminaries, etc., devoted to the teaching of theology. Some distinctions need to be made, but first I have a terminological proposal.

It is frequent for a study to take the name of what it is a study *of*, or at least for the two to have the same name (for we must remember that sometimes the aspect of the world takes its name from the study; thus the geography of Lapland is a chunk of the earth's surface, etc., defined, so to say, by the interest of the geographer). Sometimes the use of the magic ending '-ology' and its sisters shows that we are talking about the study of the thing not the thing (as in 'theology'). In English we have no easy way of tacking on the equivalent of *Wissenschaft*, so we tend to be landed with cumbrous titles

11

like 'the study of religion' and 'Religious Studies'; while in the world of pedagogy the fashion is to use 'Religious Education', concealing some thoughtful ambiguities in the adjective. In America conciseness has won the day in universities: there are Departments of Religion, *tout court.* Just as one who teaches (researches into) Politics or Government is not except perchance actually a politician or governor, so one who teaches (researches into) Religion is not necessarily religious in any particular tradition, etc. Strictly, I suppose, Religion ought to have 'and Atheism, etc.' tacked on to it. The American usage in this respect is the one I shall employ here: instead of writing of 'the study of religion', I shall refer to 'Religion'. The capital can serve to distinguish the study from what it is a study *of*, namely religion.

Apart from lack of cumbrousness, the title has a great advantage over its succinct alternative, 'theology'. The latter term is silent about its necessary adjective. It is usually taken to mean Christian theology, but there are, obviously, other kinds – Jewish, Muslim, and so forth. Worse, some other traditions could not use the term, though their 'theologians' might be engaged in a similar enterprise to that of Christian ones. For instance, the Theravada Buddhist does not believe in a Theos, so how can he do theology? Buddhology or dhammology might be his equivalent activity. Another ambiguity lurking in the current usage of 'theology' is that between theology conceived as historical, philological, scientific study (in this sense it is part of Religion) and theology conceived as the *expression* in systematic or learned form of the faith of a tradition. The latter enterprise can be conceived as a sort of preaching, as a re-presentation of the Gospel (or the Dhamma, etc.), or at least as the assembling of materials for preaching. Such theology is positional rather than descriptive–scientific: that is, it expresses a position in a given tradition, or anti-tradition. To say that it is not descriptive–scientific in main intent (though it obviously must use the materials furnished by Religion) is not to criticise it, merely to make a distinction. But we shall see that there are questions about the distinction. So far it can only be taken as a rough approximation, but one which can however form the basis of a further terminological

12

proposal. Let us call the activity of expressing a position, *Expression*, one form of which is Christian Theology (the capital 'T' can signify that we are here considering Theology in its main intent, and not the descriptive–scientific ancillaries which often go under the name of theology, such as the history of Israel). The suggestion of the present argument and proposals is that Expression is not part of the study of Religion, but this as we shall discover is an oversimplification.

Since Theology has been typically the mother of Religion in the universities of the West, some light upon the programme of exploring religion may be gained by examining the common anatomy of theological disciplines. A critique of that anatomy will pave the way for a fuller description of the structure of Religion. After that, we can look at the religious world of which Religion can be a mirror and sketch out a characterisation of religion.

Consider a common spectrum of studies designed for the education of the Christian Theologian [3]: Old Testament, New Testament, patristics, Church history, history of doctrine, liturgiology, Christian ethics (moral theology), pastoral theology, systematic theology (dogmatic theology), missiology, philosophy of religion, comparative study of religion (history of religions, phenomenology of religion), religious sociology. Every one of these branches of the subject displays overlaps and ambiguities.

Consider first the study of the Old Testament. At one level it can be simply the unravelling of the history of Israel in the context of its environment, and it presumably needs to be carried on through the inter-testamental period if it is to form a continuous background to the New Testament period. Part of this exploration will reveal the Theologies or Theology expressed in the O.T. and more generally in early Judaism, and the moral values espoused there. Since however the O.T. and pre-Christian Judaism are assigned a certain status in the Christian tradition, it typically happens that the revealing of a Theology, so far a strictly historical enterprise, can tacitly or explicitly lead to the *endorsing* of that Theology (or at least the partial endorsing of it, for the Christian Theologian is not *totally* committed to the O.T.). The endorsing of a Theology is

13

essentially an Expression of it. Thus the study of the O.T. bifurcates into an historical and an Expressive element, the latter forming, from a logical point-of-view, part of the substance of systematic Theology and moral Theology. Similar remarks apply with even greater force to the study of the New Testament. Discovering what Paul's Theology was is strictly an historical exercise, but since the assumption of the Christian Theologian is that Paul has a rather high degree of authority, the historical exercise is liable to merge imperceptibly into that of Expression, by endorsement.

The chopping up of the history of the Judaeo-Christian tradition into various periods is not by itself logical, but tends to reflect the interests of Theologians, that is to reflect assumptions about the historical loci of Theological, moral, and liturgical developments deemed to have special authority. Hence the patristic period tends to be separated off, and for Protestants, the Reformation also. From a purely scientific point-of-view it would be more satisfactory to consider the Judaeo-Christian tradition as a continuous whole, though bifurcating after the time of Jesus into on-going Judaism and Christianity. The history of Christianity, as that of other religions, could be treated as containing differing strands or dimensions: doctrinal, liturgical, moral, institutional, etc. Naturally the understanding of developments in the differing dimensions would have to be done in context (moral and social attitudes changing with metamorphoses in the institutions, and so on). All this body of history, and especially doctrinal, liturgical, and ethical aspects thereof, could then be used if so desired as material to endorse or otherwise use in the Expressive tasks of systematic Theology, moral Theology, liturgical prescription, and so on.

A terminological proposal arising from this is that it is rather unwise to use the term 'Church history' (or 'ecclesiastical history'), for the following reasons. (i) The determinants of religious changes do not wholly lie within the body identified as 'the Church'. (ii) To identify some institution or institutions as the Church is liable to involve endorsing a given Theology of the Church, that is to go beyond history. (iii) It is cumbrous to invent parallel titles for other faiths, such as Sanghic history

14

(for Buddhism). It is surely easier to speak of the history of Christianity and of the history of Buddhism.

All this would signify that the history of Christianity, together with the Judaism often incorporated into theological syllabuses, is correctly to be viewed as part of the history of religions (that is, part of what commonly also goes under the unfortunate title 'comparative study of religion').

Since Theological Expression is both doctrinal and practical, the materials of many disciplines, not just of the history of Christianity, can be used to make prescriptions. Thus materials from the psychology of religion (itself drawing on the history and phenomenology of religious experience) can be used in pastoral Theology; materials drawn from social history and sociology of religion (which is in principle scientific not Expressive) can be used to do religious sociology, which is prescriptively oriented; materials from the history and phenomenology of religion can be used in missiology. Since these branches of Theology are in the end Expressive, and presuppose a position in the tradition, however radically it may be developing, their titles are all essentially elliptical. One should speak of *Christian* moral, pastoral, social, and missiological Theology. There can be parallel Expressive activities in other faiths. But there are elements in all these studies, the 'materials' of which I have spoken, which properly fall under the scientific study, Religion.

It remains to say something of the rather peculiar position of the philosophy of religion. It is liable to include discussions of natural theology and in this it exhibits its membership of systematic Theology (never mind whether a person believes in natural theology or not: the thesis that none of the proofs of God's existence works, or that Aquinas' doctrine of analogy is defective or that natural theology is incompatible with an endorsed Pauline doctrine of grace – all are systematic Theological points-of-view). Philosophy of religion is also liable to be concerned with questions of compatibility and of criteria of truth and falsity: to this extent it goes beyond systematic Theology, though it is relevant to it. It is not Expressing, but saying something about the rules of Expression. Since, however, many Theologies incorporate judgements (perhaps they

15

all ought to?) about the rules of Expression, if only by appeal to authority, it is indeed hard to maintain a strong distinction between Theological and philosophical debates. However, a theoretical distinction can remain, for philosophical debates are relevant also to questions of the relations between Theological Expressions and the human sciences, such as psychology of religion, and of the relations between Theologies of differing faiths. To the problem of the status of the philosophy of religion we shall return.

Meanwhile the critique of the anatomy of theological studies can be briefly summed up as follows: that we always need to make a distinction between historical and structural enquiries, such as sociology, phenomenology, etc., which are the proper province of Religion, and the *use* of such materials for Expressive ends, that is, the doing of Theology. The critique implies that some restrictions and inconsistencies have been placed upon scientific studies by the needs of Expression. Once, however, the distinction between doing Religion and doing Theology (e.g., Christian Theology) has been clearly made, the troubles occasioned by confusing the two seem to evaporate. (Or at least they become other sorts of troubles, such as the problem of whether a secular State ought to subsidise Theology and so on.)

But perhaps I am over-hopeful, or disingenuous. After all, I have skated over some thin ice. Two immediate reactions are liable to be evoked by the distinction: (i) is it ever really possible to be 'scientific', that is, free from a position which is tacitly or otherwise Expressed and which determines the shape and conclusions of one's study of religion? I am doubtless especially prone to this counter, having included the study of non-religious ideologies as an adjunct to Religion; (ii) one aspect of the hermeneutical problem is this: can there be an 'objective' or uncommitted understanding of what it is that a given religion is about? Both questions bristle with difficulties.

(i) A modest first move to deal with the implied objection is to ask: What sort of freedom from Expression is it that we are supposed to be unable to attain? Is the claim being made that *as a matter of fact* (humans being what they are) everyone is

16

somewhat biased by his convictions when it comes to dealing with religion? To this I reply: first, there are degrees of bias: some omnipresent bias does not legitimate universal great bias; and second, more importantly, does a scholar's position *legitimately* influence his conclusions in this sphere? In the latter case there has to be some logical or intrinsic connection between his beliefs and his role as explorer of religion. Otherwise, the lament that men are liable to weaknesses and distortions which impede their goals is an old one: we know that men are imperfect, but they can become *better* at doing things if they set their hearts on it. (One thing they could do is to leave the study of religion to those who are least inclined to bias!) The objection, then, can only hold if there is a logical connection between the scholar's position and the kind of conclusion he ought to arrive at. One way in which there might be such a logical connection is hinted at in question (ii), namely that understanding presupposes faith, etc. Before turning to this question, let us briefly note a feature of the intellectual firmament.

At a given time, and sometimes more continuously and for deep-seated reasons, an issue may be highly *debatable*. Quite clearly some issues are more debatable than others. For example, there is scarcely room for debate that the earth is roughly spherical; on the other hand, there is much room for debate as to the most effective way of trying to solve the international monetary problems of the Western world. An issue may be debatable for a number of reasons: often the evidence is not easy to make precise, or is grossly lacking (and perhaps must be so, as for example when we make untried social arrangements which can only be evaluated in the future). The greater the debatability of an issue the more one is liable to get intuitive judgements (seeing the situation as X rather than Y, and so on), and also for that matter emotionally-influenced judgements. This in itself is no bad thing, for if an issue cannot easily be resolved one still may have to come to a conclusion, and summing things up intuitively is doubtless better than tossing a coin (it could only be worse, I suppose, if constitutionally humans tended intuitively to go for unrealistic, perhaps wish-fulfilling, judgements, but this thesis itself is one of the

17

highly debatable ones!) One would thus expect that debatable issues are more easily influenced by positions, by tacit Expressions of *Weltanschauungen*, than those where the methodology and the evidences are more precise. But what are the things that are debatable in the ambit of Religion? Let us consider two issues, and comment.

(*a*) It is unclear precisely what the religion of the Indus Valley civilisation involved: for example, was some form of yoga practised [4]? (There are lots of analogous queries about ancient religions.) *Comment*: there is a dearth of literary/oral tradition capable of resolving the question, in the light of the present archaeological evidence. That is what you expect with some ancient cultures, but similar problems arise about marriage institutions, methods of tending cattle, and so forth. It is not a problem peculiar to *religion*.

(*b*) Whether there was any close connection between the Protestant Reformation and the rise of capitalism is debatable. *Comment*: it is debatable because we cannot experiment with whole societies and with unique historical sequences (necessarily), while the evidence is so complex, vast and at the same time incomplete that the best we can say is that much of it is *suggestive* of the Weberian thesis. Much of historical sociology is like this and bound to be. How would a religious position affect one's approach? It would affect it by making one take religious factors more *seriously*, not treating religion as a mere epiphenomenon. One could take this position, though, without Expressing a given tradition; treating religion seriously is not, then, *logically* dependent on Expressing a tradition.

Here then are two cases of debatable issues. But what of matters more directly of faith? It may be that an Expression of faith is necessarily debatable but I hope to have shown that because an issue relating to religion is debatable it does not follow that it is intrinsically determined by Expression of faith (by a Theology). If there is to be a logical, intrinsic reason for holding that Expression tacitly or explicitly pervades every serious exploration of a religious tradition, it must be that the understanding of a tradition presupposes some kind of acceptance, that is, we now turn to the problem posed in question (ii).

18

There might be several explanations of why acceptance is necessary to understanding.

(*a*) To understand myths and doctrines it is necessary to participate in the rites which are coordinated with them: for example, Christology is related to the sacraments.

(*b*) To understand what myths and doctrines refer to it is necessary to have some experience of their Focus (what they point to): for example, you cannot understand the meaning of Christology without experiencing the risen Christ.

(*c*) What the faith essentially means is what it means today; this cannot be expressed without Expressing it.

Because some very profound questions arise from (*c*), I shall discuss this first, and in some detail. I am not, incidentally, claiming that the three reasons above given for the necessity of acceptance for understanding are either exhaustive or mutually exclusive. To discuss the issue posed under (*c*) it is necessary to set up a model of a religious tradition, and for ease of recourse to examples I shall take the case of Christianity (but with its features necessarily simplified).

Looked at from the human end, Christianity comprises a population of believers (and on the edges half-believers), organised into an institution which for the sake of simplicity we shall call the Church (ignoring for now denominational and national divisions). The institution has visible expression in its rituals and buildings and in the formal and informal behaviour of its members. To understand their behaviour, especially formal behaviour (for example, when engaged in sacramental ritual, hymn-singing or prayer) and to understand their mutual loyalty in the institution, it is necessary to pay attention to the beliefs held, notably those which are institutional, that is, held not merely as private beliefs but as defining the institution. As well as being ethical, these beliefs are also both doctrinal and what I shall call mythic. By 'mythic' beliefs I refer to those which refer to the story of divine action, notably in Christ. By doctrines I mean the analyses of the nature of the transcendent (e.g., the Trinity doctrine), which typically arise out of and in relation to the mythic beliefs. By ethical beliefs, I refer to the beliefs about general conduct and about the right form of society which are held to flow from acceptance of the doctrines

19

and myths in the context of the ritual (liturgical) life of the institution. The experiences of Christians in this whole context are held to be experiences *of* that to which the doctrines, myths, and ethical beliefs point and to which worship is directed. Although the sense of 'reference' shifts in the different dimensions of the religious tradition, we can loosely say that the different aspects of the life of those who belong to the institution refer to (point to, are directed at) a Focus (God or God in Christ, etc.) [5].

Thus singing a hymn, acting in a certain way, evolving a Theology, testifying, painting a picture, and designing a religious building, all these can be ways of Expressing something about the Focus. We shall call a given set of such Expressions a *picture* of the Focus (the thought being, incidentally, that where the picture does justice to the Focus the Focus is present in the picture, that is in the lives of Christians). Again to simplify, we shall assume that each age has a dominant collective picture of the Focus. Needless to say this simplification moves far from the facts, but a relatively simple model to begin with may help to unravel some of the complexities of the hermeneutical problem posed by suggestion (*c*) above.

Let us now crudely define an age as a century, and let the centuries run appropriately from I to XX. The dominant picture of a century can, for example, be styled thus: 'The I-picture' (the first century picture). Now we are in a position to ask some questions about understanding the Focus and about understanding the pictures. There are of course some built-in limits to understanding the Focus, for it would be part of all the pictures in the Christian gallery that the Focus is in part beyond human comprehension. But we can neglect this point, for surely what is being asked for is not perfect understanding but as good as a man of faith can expect, or as good a one as might pass for adequate. For, after all, the suggestion of (*c*) is that without expression the Religionist cannot adequately understand Christianity; that is, the suggestion is that if he is not a Christian he is worse off, and the criteria of being a Christian may be rather humble ones. What then is it to understand the Focus adequately? We might answer: by selecting the picture which does most justice to the Focus.

20

But how do we know this? And how do we *select* precisely (for selecting is Expressing, is it not?) One criterion might be that all the pictures had in common a respect for the authority of the I-picture, so this would be the one to uncover. This is the motive for discovering and endorsing a New Testament Theology. But a number of problems arise immediately: in uttering a New Testament Theology (e.g., Paul's Theology) am I actually Expressing the I-picture? The reason for doubt is that the terms I use have a new significance in *my* twentieth-century milieu. For example, if I affirm a miracle in this scientific age am I *making the same point* as was originally being made? We may call this the phenomenon of milieu-transformation. Milieu-transformation implies that the more things stay the same the more they change (over time and as between cultures). It seems then that I am in a predicament: I wish to Express the I-picture, but end up Expressing something different; yet on the other hand one thread running through the gallery of Christian pictures is that the I-picture has some authority and is in fact in substance identical with the later pictures Expressed (or at least with the one which is being Expressed).

One attempted solution to the problem is to employ an analogical method: if the I-picture is like this, then given the difference in cultural milieu between then and now, we construct a XX-picture which will do justice to the Focus and will thus in spirit be identical to the I-picture. But notice a secret assumption of this analogical approach: it is that it is possible to *delineate* the I-picture in relation to its cultural milieu. It is not a matter here of directly attempting to Express the I-picture, for this attempt would collapse under milieu-transformation. The analogical approach certainly does not support the thesis that *acceptance* is necessary to understanding. The work of uncovering the I-picture in the first instance is a matter of sensitive scientific enquiry, not of Expression. This signalises the way in which *every past picture* itself can become the object of scientific enquiry. Or to put it another way, every attempt to employ a past Expression as an Expression makes it into a form of contemporary Expression. However, this preliminary conclusion needs to be modified (as we shall) for we still have not fully explored the question of the continuity of dominant pictures from I to XX. Let us approach this problem obliquely by considering what is meant by the question: 'What is Christianity'? [6]

The banal answer, that it is a religion professed by so many million people and going back to Jesus, has its uses, of course. It refers to actual Christianity as embodied in people and institutions and hardware. But we also want to say something like this: that actual Christianity rarely expresses true Christianity (let us not bother with whether this judgement is correct – it is a possible thing to say). In our jargon, this means something like this: that the dominant picture of the twentieth century does not do justice to the Focus or more radically that few of the dominant pictures, if any, have done justice to the Focus. But this itself is to Express a picture of the Focus. It makes no sense to say that other pictures have not presented true Christianity (the true Faith) unless a picture of the Truth is available, that is, available through Expression. It is another matter to claim that the one who makes such an Expression in criticism of most or all of the rest of Christianity is right; we are at the moment concerned with what he is *doing*, and what he is doing is Expressing a picture of the Focus of Christianity. (There is, perhaps, a marginal problem here, namely what the bounds of Christianity are, but to that I return in any case.)

One might here make a distinction between two general types of Expressers of Christianity, the traditional and the prophetic. No value judgement is implied here, firstly because though prophets tend to be highly regarded there can be false prophets; secondly because though traditionalists are often condemned there can be good traditions; and thirdly because in any case I am commenting from a higher point-of-view ('higher' that is in logical level, attempting to describe forms of Expression rather than to Express my own reaction to them). The traditional type of Expression affirms solidarity with a large number of preceding pictures. The prophetic type attacks many preceding (and even contemporary) pictures. The one says: 'I agree with what pictures I to XIX were getting at: I re-Express the point of view delineated in the tradition as follows. . . .' Naturally in reality there are varia-

22

tions on this theme; remember that I have been using a simplified, homogenised model of the Christian tradition. Variations one could point to in reality are such as this: the Catholic Theologian who affirms the values of the Catholic tradition, in the manner which I've called traditionalist, even though for example it may turn out that the dominant picture of XIX is Protestant. But our traditionalist ignores this motif, for his eyes are fixed, naturally enough, on the Roman Catholic strand. The difference between the traditionalist and the prophetic type can be crudely delineated as follows: the former is more willing to make a *collage* of pictures I to XIX. His willingness arises from this fact, that he Expresses solidarity with the continuity of pictures. For one thing, he formally identifies with at least the *intention* of the tradition, namely to Express a true picture of the Focus. This tends to lead materially to the subsumption in his own picture of elements drawn from the total tradition. Naturally, our traditionalist is himself a model, just as our account of Christianity has been a simplified model. This is what I mean, then, by the tendency of the traditionalist to produce a *collage*. He arranges the pictures of earlier centuries, but of course their meaning is changed due to milieu-transformation; but then the *collage* itself provides each picture with a milieu different from its earlier single frame. Actually, by extension, some of the earlier pictures themselves were of the *collage* kind; now they are micro-*collages* subsumed into a macro-*collage*, which itself could in principle serve as an element in a further *collage* in ages yet to come.

I referred earlier to a banal answer to the question of what is Christianity. A slightly more sophisticated one is available, namely a tradition institutionalised in such and such a way and going back to Jesus, held by such and such a number of people in such and such a number of countries, etc., who have presented dominant pictures of the Focus to which their activities are directed (insofar as they take the Focus seriously), namely pictures I to XX. The more sophisticated answer exhibits the building in which the collection of pictures is housed and the range of pictures themselves. The traditionalist type of Christian has himself a picture which can correspond

23

reasonably closely to the more sophisticated (but still banal) description of what Christianity is. His *collage* has a correspondence because the new description of Christianity, though not Expressive, exhibits the range of pictures. This was how Christianity was initially, Expressing this picture; then it was like this; and so on. Needless to say there are complications which we can for the moment ignore. After all, the traditionalist may not know what the *actual* III-picture was, so that his III-picture is better put as 'III, as seen from the perspective of the twentieth-century traditionalist'. The traditionalist's pictures may thus differ subtly or even grossly from the historian's; and again the traditionalist may not be quite impartially catholic in his tastes – he may stress the XIII-picture much more than others, pasting as it were a bigger picture of Aquinas on the wall than that of John Scotus. Still, his answer to the question 'What is Christianity?' (i.e., 'Please Express it') may bear a not-too-distant relationship to the historian's answer to the question (now meaning 'Please describe it'). This correspondence may not be perfect, but is likely to be greater than that between the historian's answer and that of the prophetic type. This may be one reason why the traditionalist is more patient of Religion than the prophetic type. The more the tradition is challenged the less relevant seems the historical answer to the question of what is (or what has been) Christianity. (But one should note the question's essential ambiguity.)

The fact that the traditionalist's account of history, for example, of the I-picture, may not correspond to the historian's, or rather to the Religionist's (he is concerned with uncovering the picture Expressed by first-century Christians and its milieu) adds a complication to the scene. The Religionist in describing the I-picture (a debatable exercise, incidentally, as we all know) has to bear in mind that the traditionalist or prophetic Christian in the twentieth century may have a different account of the I-picture, so that in penetrating to the I-picture he is not at all necessarily uncovering what the I-picture *means* to the twentieth-century Christian.

This complication, of the difference between history as it was and history as it is perceived, affects the question of what is Christianity, for from the point-of-view of describing a twentieth-century Expression of Christianity it is the I-picture as perceived which is important. Fortunately, this tension is mitigated by the fact that much of twentieth-century Christianity is aware of the reflexive effects of Religion, and attempts to incorporate a scientific account of the I-picture into its XX Expressive picture. Incidentally, if one wanted to go to town on symbolism (and it would probably do no harm, as symbolism is one of our best devices for sorting out what is complex) one would have to invent such symbolisms as: 'XIX (I-picture) picture', meaning the dominant account of the first-century picture endorsed in the dominant twentieth-century picture' – perhaps the Jesus of Liberal Theology. If one wanted to particularise, one would invent: 'Barth's (Paul's picture) picture'. *Question*: was Paul's picture equivalent to Barth's (Paul's picture) picture?

The tone of this question, though, seems to leave something out. The hermeneutical problem is deeper than suspected and not capable of resolution simply by making the distinction between description and Expression, however sophisticatedly (for example, by noting that past Expression can be described; that descriptive materials can be used in Expression; that there is an assimilation of the results of Religion into the making of Theology; that Christianity consists in an institution housing a gallery of Expressive pictures, now to be described; that the past is seen in the tradition not necessarily as it happened, and so forth). For the question 'What is Christianity?' *even at the descriptive level* is bound up closely with the ongoing activity of Expression. How is this? At the risk of a little distortion, let us make an analogy with a person, not yet dead, and consider who he is: for the question of the nature of Christianity is a bit like that of the character of a person.

If you ask: 'Who is Roncalli?' (let us suppose him not yet dead) you might get answers along the lines that he has lately been elected Pope. That identifies him, but what *sort* of man is he? Well, he is fat, bonhomous, ascetic in his way, no mean intellect, has ecumenical interests, comes from North Italian peasant stock, is shrewd, old, probably a stop-gap. All this

25

seems to tell you what he is like, but you do not *really* know. You will have to see how he reacts to his new situation in the Papacy.

The example, I hope, is reasonably perspicuous. It was, as it turned out, in his last years that Roncalli showed most obviously his character. Perhaps some of his actions could have been anticipated; there is no need to deny this. All that I here emphasise is that no complete or satisfactory answer to the question 'What sort of man is Roncalli?' could have been given just after his election to the Papacy. The Roncalli in question was a developing Roncalli. There is no reason in principle to treat a collective tradition differently from an individual. If Christianity includes a gallery, it is a growing gallery of pictures; it could be that future pictures could throw light on the preceding sequence. The collection changes, even its existing members change in a way, when a new member is added. Thus a final answer (even from the point-of-view of Religion) to the question: 'What is Christianity?' cannot be given.

This conclusion is reinforced by some considerations about meaning. Consider the nature of belief: it would generally be regarded today as clear that a belief is a disposition (though a disposition to 'do' what would be in dispute); it would also be agreed that a belief typically is expressible in words, for example in a statement. Some statements are not very precise, but they can still express beliefs, and the disposition has then some considerable latitude in the directions of its manifestations. Thus in such a case if you ask someone what he believes you can get an answer in words. But the full account of what he believes is not revealed until he makes later moves under the rubric of the disposition. What he believes points to the future; exactly what he believes is revealed therein. For example, I say that I believe that Jonathan is reliable, he'll back you up when you're in trouble. Later I am in trouble and drop a line to Jonathan. He fails to turn up at the meeting place I suggested. A friend says: 'So he's not reliable after all.' 'Yes he is,' I answer. 'But he can occasionally be absent-minded.' 'Despite this, then, you still believe he is reliable?' 'Yes,' I say; my belief has not changed but it has gained a

26

qualification. I endorse the old belief as being the same, though I had not then thought of the qualification which would have to be made. It is a bit like a sequence of moves at chess. The later moves belong to the one I initiated, even if I have had to modify my plan.

Sometimes we are tempted into a converse judgement about the identity of a belief with one held in the past. When I was a child, dutifully closing my eyes during the Lord's Prayer, and having heard it said that the power of the Holy Spirit is released through prayer, I believed that the murmuring sound all about was indeed the Spirit working. Later, having found that it was the low voice of many folk joining in the prayer, I might still utter the same words, but does my belief amount to the *same* belief? It is tempting to say that it is not. The only point on the other side would have to be expressed rather like this: 'As a child you thought that the Holy Spirit was specially present in the church, and this was essentially correct.' This would be, I suppose, a way of affirming the solidarity of my present belief with the intention of those who taught me as a child; a kind of adoption of an earlier (surely different?) belief as essentially the same as that which I hold now. The question such examples pose is: 'What are the criteria of identity of belief?' Given that there is typically some latitude, an open texture in the disposition defined by the words, how much can the words be stretched and reinterpreted? How loose can the fit between two sets of words be?

There is an analogous problem in the question of the 'essential' identity of the pictures presented in the gallery of Christian Expression. However, the important conclusion in the meantime is that a belief has a *future* outreach (as does a living man's character). Hence the present Expression of Christianity may clarify its nature in the future, and this latitude may allow it to merge into a rather different picture in XXI. Hence the question (descriptively) 'What is Christianity?' cannot wholly be answered by exhibiting the gallery of existing pictures in the institutional building which houses them.

Since what a belief is can emerge in the future with greater clarity, it follows that a present, more defined and articulated belief can throw light on what it once was, before the later moves were made. It is by no means absurd to claim that though X asserted p at t_1 what he was trying to say was pq (save that it was only at t_2 the means were available to assert 'q'). A dangerous doctrine, no doubt, for it could lend a handle to those who wish to bend wills and to betray old commitments. Nevertheless, it is a doctrine which arises naturally from the fact that people or traditions with living pasts, that is, with pasts that still enter into present activities, can see a consistency in the development of their ideas.

Thus to return to the analogy of the gallery of pictures, a new picture added may reveal something about the existing collection; it may bring something out not so clearly seen before. In this sense the new work throws light on the old, but without necessarily challenging the old we are still moving within the model of the traditionalist approach; the prophetic type will have his moment shortly, and similar considerations apply in his case). In this sense, the question (descriptively) 'What is Christianity?' is not finally settled, for some changes can occur which would modify the description of the existing gallery of Expressive pictures. Description then has to recognise the ongoing character of certain religious traditions; to that extent description remains provisional, like a biography of a man still living.

A conclusion to be drawn from this is that there is a parallel to the reflexive effect of Religion upon Theology. As we mentioned earlier, descriptive studies of a religious tradition, etc., may themselves have an effect upon the way in which Theology sees the past; such knowledge is taken up into new forms of Expression. Conversely it is in principle possible for new forms of Expression to play a part in revising judgements in Religion, not merely because a new Expression is a further fact in the ongoing history of a tradition, but also because it may cast light upon the past.

However, this by no means entails that it is necessary to Express in order to do Religion. Rather, it entails that the Religionist must be able to discuss and engage with the Theologians of the traditions with which he is concerned. This is a cumbrous way of saying that Religion should not cut itself off from sensitive contact with the living exponents of faiths.

28

All this argument has been on the assumption of a certain continuity in the gallery of pictures. But the prophetic type may not see things thus. For him a number of the pictures belonging to the gallery hitherto labelled 'Christianity' need to be *rejected* as failing to reflect the Focus. This is a stronger repudiation than the recognition, perhaps shared by everyone in the tradition, that every picture is partially defective. Let us consider briefly three (not necessarily incompatible) forms of the prophetic type, which I shall label 'biblical', 'experiential', and 'ethical'.

The biblical type could be represented, in our terms, as holding that a number of the pictures in the gallery are incompatible with the I-picture, taken as normative. The experiential type holds that his own (or his and his fellows') experience of the Focus leads to the rejection of some of the pictures. The ethical type holds that some of the pictures are in conflict with the main emphasis of Christian moral values. Now a feature of all these positions is that they are selective as among the pictures; even in the case of the experiential type, the very notion that he has experience of the Focus implies that he accepts some picture of the Focus from the tradition as connected to his experience (for otherwise he cannot even say: 'This is how Christ really means us to act', etc.). All the cases are selective acceptance-and-criticism of the tradition. By using the word 'selective' here I am not meaning to imply that there is something arbitrary about it, nor am I denying that from a Theological point-of-view the selection may be Expressed as election.

The prophetic picture, then, is one which recognises its inner connection with some of the pictures, I and following, but affirms its incompatibility with others. But this of course only shows one way in which our original simplified model of the tradition was over-simplified. For of course the tradition has actually been broken up over long periods into different institutional groups with rather different and often seemingly conflicting pictures, so that one could not for example talk of a single XVII-picture, but rather of XVII*a*, XVII*b*, XVII*c*, XVII*d* . . . pictures (e.g., Roman Catholic, Lutheran, Anabaptist, Russian Orthodox . . .). Crudely, the prophetic picture

29

is one version of the XX collection. This extra complication, however, does not radically affect our argument for a dialectical relation between Religion and Expression, though it does raise a further question about 'What is Christianity?'

In effect the prophetic stance treats some pictures in the tradition as merely *claiming* Christian pedigree without having a right to it. Can then these pictures be included within the history of Christianity, properly speaking? Likewise, what is to be said of ancient heresies, for they claimed to be Christian even if ultimately condemned by the catholic body. The answer to the problem, from the point-of-view of Religion, is two-fold. First, there is no obstacle in all this to a treatment, historically, phenomenologically and otherwise, of the whole family-tree of movements, sects, denominations, etc., springing originally from the early church; such a treatment can bring out the ways each Expresses its faith and its acceptance or non-acceptance of other movements, sects, etc. Second, there is the need to reaffirm the ambiguity of the question 'What is Christianity?': in one sense this is asking for Expression, in another it is asking for a description of the main features of the Christian tradition developing up to and through the present day. The latter question is what is answered by Religion, as we have seen, in dialogue with Theological Expression. The answer of Religion requires debatable judgement of course, for some fringe prophetic group may be deemed as too distant in spirit from main-stream Christianities to warrant a place in the Christian tradition; yet such a judgement could turn out to be wrong, through, for example, developments in the group showing a more dynamic and intimate interplay with aspects of the tradition than at first suspected (developments which might alter one's appraisal of the meaning or the original prophecy). There is certainly no way in which Religion can claim to be other than revisionary in principle about its judgements, in line with any other form of intellectual exploration.

Now we may return to the other arguments which might be used to back the thesis that acceptance is a necessary condition of properly understanding a faith. To sum up the main conclusion arising from the question of Expression, it is that

30

the Religionist requires to enter into engagement with those who carry on the Expression of the faith, though this does not entail that he is thereby chiefly concerned with Expression. But more will be said about this conclusion once we have briefly adverted to the other arguments. One of them, to repeat, was this:

(*a*) To understand myths and doctrines it is necessary to participate in the rites which are coordinated to them. For example, Christology is related to the sacraments.

Though this is an important point, I do not wish to spend much time on it here. Briefly, the main comments are these: first, accepting the principle of the coordination between doctrines and myths on the one hand and rites and practice on the other, though it is true that one would need to know what for example worship involves, that is one would need to have a general understanding of the category of practices involved, it does not follow that one would need to be committed to the particular practices in question (though see the answer to the next argument (*b*) for a modification of this view). Second, the difficulty is not felt all that acutely by anthropologists – who are commonly in the position of participant observation. Nor is it a difficulty felt so acutely by those who learn from literature – I may not share the beliefs and values of Father Zossima in 'The Brothers Karamazov', but I can (so to say) 'act his part'. An important feature of human capacities is that we can use imagination and empathy as well as reasoning powers.

The other argument was this:

(*b*) To understand what myths and doctrines refer to it is necessary to have some experience of their Focus (what they point to). For example you cannot understand the meaning of Christology without experiencing the risen Christ.

A battery of problems emerges here: first, is the point about the experience of the Focus its *particularity*? To turn to a 'secular' example, I may know what love is like (I love my wife), but does this precisely tell me what it is *like* for Onassis to love Jackie? The answer probably is: with sufficient imagination I can gain some understanding of what it is like. The function of the novelist and the biographer is in part to expand our imaginations of the particular, and there is no reason in principle why Religion should not do the same (though literary techniques have probably been under-developed in this field.

Second, is the point about experience of the Focus that it somehow gets *behind* the pictures which are Expressed about the Focus? Clearly it must be that in some sense the experience does. But there are also necessary limitations on the Expression of the experience, that is, this is not just a problem for Religion but also for Theology: the expression of what an experience is like does not necessarily convey it. Further, from an institutional point-of-view there is no guarantee of any equal or similar experience of the Focus among the adherents, and yet the Theology or picture of the Focus is in a degree publicly shared. Consequently, there is intrinsically liable to be a gap between experience and public Expression.

Third, is the point about experience that it needs expressive, not just descriptive, treatment? Here we come to a vital point in the whole argument as to the relation between Religion and Expression. The question asks in effect whether a neutral description can bring out such things as the joy found in the experience of the risen Christ – joy which might be expressed in traditional religious terms by 'Alleluiah!' or by the outpouring of spirit in a victorious hymn (e.g., 'Jesus Christ is risen today', as sung at Easter) or by joyful behaviour in general.

This suggests a comment which has been implicit in the account hitherto given here of what Expression and a picture amount to. It is that we are not solely concerned with *beliefs* (e.g., in doctrines or myths); we are not solely concerned with matters of *truth*, but also of value, feeling, ritual, etc. In phenomenological exploration it is not possible to confine the *epoche* (to use Husserl's jargon) to suspend judgement as to the *truth* of what is being investigated. The bracketing must also be a bracketing of expressions of value, feeling, etc. This point can be brought out by considering the familiar linguistic device of *oratio obliqua*. Thus 'George said that the moon is volcanic' does not commit one to the belief that the moon is volcanic but it does succeed in conveying (if my statement is true) what George's belief is. Consider now: 'George said that sending

32

rockets to the moon is a bloody waste of money.' Equally I am not committed to his value judgement. With a bit of acting, to get the right fire into what comes after 'George said that . . .' I can convey the tone of George's utterance and through it the feeling expressed by him. It is common for us in such 'oblique' situations to act out another's utterance and reactions. This is necessarily so where we are primarily concerned to get across what it was *like* for the person in question in a particular situation (and/or what it was like for the 'reporter', reacting to the other in the situation). Some 'flat' descriptions largely fail: thus 'George's foot was blown off by the grenade; he fell over and, bleeding rather, addressed some remarks to the Virgin Mary' could be bettered, if one were wanting to bring out George's agony in the situation.

Now the project of bringing out what a situation is *like* is important in trying to convey the content of religious perception and of religious practice. This does not commit oneself to that content or to those feelings (just as the novelist and biographer brings out the feelings of characters with whom he does not necessarily identify, a self-critical sympathy being, however, some advantage). Thus religious phenomenology requires not merely the *oratio obliqua* of beliefs *that,* but a bracketing of all that is being presented. This presentation, however, within brackets, uses many of the elements of Expression, not just doctrinal statements. Thus an important part of description is what may be called 'bracketed Expression'.

One may ask, however, what the point is of using bracketed Expression when Expression alone would do. This is to misunderstand the situation. The Religionist is concerned with those who Express faith, but not with giving personal testimony. In his bracketing he is parasitic upon the Expresser, obviously; his advantage only is that he can survey a broad range of religious facts, and this is not the primary aim of, and often is not within the competence of, the Expresseer. Put crudely: a saint can be poor at Religion; and Napoleon could have been a poor biographer.

So, then, the fact that experience of the Focus may require Expression in terms of feeling and value does not entail that it cannot be handled in some degree by Religion, through

33

bracketed Expression. Phenomenology needs to be evocative as well as descriptive (and it is possible to be misleading in both modes). Thus the neutralism of phenomenological enquiry aimed at revealing the content of religious pictures is not 'flat' neutralism, that is, it should not engage in those deflationary and wooden descriptions which destroy the evocative. This is a common pitfall, for an overly 'external' (that is non-evocative) account of a religious practice, mood or commitment can so easily have the effect of destroying any sense of its *impact*, and thus is lost a major aspect of its meaning.

The conclusion of this discussion of the problem of objectivity in Religion can be briefly summed up by saying that Religion incorporates, by bracketing, Expressions into its descriptions, and that there is no strong reason to hold that particular commitment is necessary to the practice of Religion. (Particular commitment is no bar either, provided it is correctly suspended, to avoid introducing Expressive judgements on the phenomena.) Perhaps I have over-laboured the question of commitment, partly by reaction against conservative criticisms of Religion, especially the so-called 'comparative study of religion', which have sometimes expressed themselves through a kind of conceptual fideism. It would doubtless be more fruitful to consider the qualities useful in a Religionist, for just as not everyone who is highly intelligent makes a good literary critic or biologist or philosopher, so there are no doubt qualities which would demarcate aptitude for Religion.

The evocative and presentative character of Religion, if done seriously, seems to be part of what Mircea Eliade has in mind in the following passage [7]:

> It seems to me difficult to believe that, living in a historical moment like ours, the historian of religions will not take account of the creative possibilities of their discipline. How to assimilate *culturally* the spiritual universes that Africa, Oceania, South-East Asia open to us? All these spiritual universes have a religious origin and structure. If one does not approach them in the perspective of the history of religions, they will disappear as spiritual universes; they will be reduced to *facts* about social organizations, economic

34

regimes, epochs of precolonial and colonial history, etc. In other words, they will not be grasped as spiritual creations; they will not enrich Western and world culture – they will serve to augment the number, already terrifying, of *documents* classified in archives, awaiting electronic computers to take them in charge.

Part of what Eliade here asks for is the communication of meanings – what I have called the evocative and presentative character of Religion. But we may note two further aspects of what he says, for they also raise questions about the relevance of Religion.

First, he seems to conceive of history of religions (Religion) as primarily a Western activity (he does not, for instance, pose the question here of how the South-East Asian is to grasp the spiritual universe of Western Christianity or Judaism), though this conception of Religion is not entirely justified historically when we consider the great contribution made by Eastern and other scholars to Religion. Nevertheless, it does force us to ask about the living milieu in which Religion operates. If Religion has the function of promoting understanding of religion, whose understanding is it? Second, there is a hint in the passage cited above of Eliade's call for a 'creative hermeneutics' in Religion, that is the presentation and development of the values of religion through the activity of the Religionist which would enable men to assimilate the meanings of religion in a new cultural self-understanding. This creative hermeneutics, if I understand it aright, would give Religion an independent dynamism as a metaphysical and cultural influence (it would seem in this way to become its own Expresser, transcending Theologies). This second aspect of Eliade's remarks raises the question of the relation of Religion to philosophy and other disciplines.

In practice the answers to the two questions posed cannot be easily disentangled. Beginning, however, at the end of the cultural milieu in which Religion is liable to operate, we must note that as an intellectual pursuit it is placed primarily in the context of scholarship and education. Its position in at least one important respect is like that of the study of literature (call this 'Literature' for short). In principle Literature transcends national boundaries: the same sort of insights can be gained, the same sorts of techniques used, by studying English and Italian literature, and the work of comparison and contrast between traditions can be illuminating, as also the work of unravelling international influences. Nevertheless, there are advantages in the student of Literature's paying *more* attention to his own tradition initially than to that of other's. Thus the balance of what may be included in Literary education, and the investment of scholarly resources as between traditions, will tend to vary from one culture to another. (More Chinese study Chinese literature than Englishmen study Chinese literature.) Likewise there is probably going to be a variation in patterns of Religion as between one culture and another, and rationally so. But this does not imply that Religion essentially differs as a pursuit from one culture to another. Here it must obey its own logic, and from that logic flows its possible contribution to education and to the wider world of human understanding.

To present its logic, however, it is necessary to say something more clearly about its anatomy than has yet been attempted in this book, drawing out some of the implications of the preceding discussion. Though I have spoken about *understanding* religious phenomena, the term needs a distinction, so let us begin with this.

Crudely, we may distinguish understanding by description (or presentation) and understanding by explanation. One task in understanding a feature of human history, etc., is understanding what it is like: to take a religious case, to understand the Roman Mass is to enter into its structure, know what it is like, know what its significance is to those who participate. This is not so far to understand how it came to be (except insofar as reference may be made within the Mass to its claimed origin). The aim of understanding by descriptive presentation is to uncover the content of a religious phenomenon.

Roughly speaking, explanations can be divided into two kinds: first, historical or narrative explanations (that is, this occurred because that occurred. For example, 'The Army posted me to Ceylon, and that was how I first came to encounter Buddhism'); and structural explanations, that is, those which appeal to some structure of reality, say human psychology. For example, 'The archetype is "that which is believed always, everywhere, and by everybody," and if it is not recognised consciously, then it appears from behind in its "wrathful" form, as the dark "son of chaos", the evil-doer, as Anti-Christ instead of Saviour . . .' [8]. We need not worry here whether this account is a *true* explanation, but it is surely the attempt to explain some features of religion through general structures of human psychology. Sometimes, of course, structural explanations are very informal and appeal to very rough generalisations ('If you spit at a man he'll get angry'); and narrative explanations continuously make appeal to structural ones ('One of the reasons why Caesar crossed the Rubicon was ambition' – it is assumed that ambition is an intelligible explanation, Caesar being the sort of person to be motivated by ambition); while structural ones themselves may have a narrative component, since structures themselves may not be universal but historically conditioned, for example, social norms. Thus the distinction between the two forms of explanation should not be taken to mean that they do not frequently combine.

Crudely, the psychology and sociology of religion aim ultimately at structural explanations, and this is why they become 'theoretical'. There is sometimes the sense here that religious phenomena are thereby being 'explained away', a general issue to which we shall return later. Briefly, the feeling is that there are psychological and sociological structures lying outside religion which are somehow more basic, so that religion can itself be explained in terms of these structures, thus becoming a mere epiphenomenon. The feeling is questionable, for the following reasons: (i) Religious institutions, etc., are part of social institutions, and if sociological explanations show (among other things) how forms of institutions have certain effects then it is hard to treat religious institutions as epiphenomenal. (ii) Similarly with psychology, religious experiences, attitudes, and so forth are part of the range of psychological phenomena, and it would be odd not to assign them 'causal' efficacy. (iii) Given that one can separate the religious from the non-religious aspects of human existence, then there is no *a priori* reason why the religious aspect should not contain its own dynamic structure about which generalisations might be made and which could in some cases help to explain non-religious events, etc. (iv) Something depends on the definition or general characterisation given to religion. (v) There are philosophical questions as to what count as alternative or competing explanations (it being commonly thought, though not necessarily correctly, that a 'naturalistic' structural explanation competes with some Theological one). In brief it is questionable, to say the least, that sociology of religion involves something called sociology lying outside religion which serves to explain the latter in terms of the former; and likewise with psychology and other related disciplines.

So far I have distinguished between description and explanation and between structural and narrative explanations. Can one speak of a structural description and a narrative description? As for the former, we may note that a religion constitutes, as it were, an organism: different elements of belief and practice affect one another's significance, and the descriptive understanding of a given feature has to take into account the organic milieu (for example, how can the Mass be understood save against the fabric of the institution of Roman Catholicism, its doctrines, ethical teachings, etc.?). So the exhibition of the meaning of a particular religious phenomenon involves placing it within a certain structure. Phenomenology of religion, therefore, has to take 'sections' of the trunk of the history of religion to exhibit the structure at a given time. We may call this activity 'structural description' (in turn, the structure may be placed in the wider structure of the society or societies in which the religion finds itself). Structural description reveals the dominant pictures of the Focus at a given time, to which we earlier referred. As for narrative description, it is a lesser element in narrative explanation, the chronicling of events rather than the giving them a coherent internal sequence.

In view of the earlier discussions of the picture-gallery, it is also possible to conceive of a structural description which does not just take sections, but indicates the way in which the sections have occurred in dynamic sequence, combining suc-

38

cessive sections in a moving phenomenological picture of a religious tradition. This would be a means of approaching the enterprise of delineating 'the spirit of Buddhism' or 'the spirit of Christianity', or whatever.

Hitherto I have tended to speak as though there is a single something, called 'religion', with which Religion is concerned. There is some point in this language, and to this I shall return. But more concretely, there are (and have been) *religions*, meaning various religious traditions and movements. Such traditions may also have a penumbra of people who do not formally belong, but have related religious concerns. Also there is the penumbra of anti-religious, atheistic, and other movements which may have something in common with religion and compete in some respects (e.g., intellectually and ethically), for example Humanism, Maoism, etc. – quasi- religions, as Tillich called them. For the moment let us briefly say, however, that the subject of Religion is religions. So in one way what is wanted first for the depiction of the anatomy of Religion is an inventory of religions.

It would be tedious to do this here in detail; a few remarks will have to suffice. First, it is best if possible to arrange the inventory according to narrative connections: thus one family tree naturally comprises Judaism, Christianity and Islam together with their offshoots, often entwined with the branches of other trees (such as the Indian tree, one of whose main branches grows into the wood of the Chinese tree and the Japanese). There may be typological reasons, to which we shall come later, why religions might be arranged according to sets of characteristics in a non-narrative inventory; but since structural descriptions will have to pay attention to the dynamic sequence of a religion's development in any case, there are important reasons initially for considering religions in an historical, narrative arrangement as far as possible.

Second, there is no great gulf fixed, from the descriptive point-of-view, between dead and living religions, save (i) that certain techniques are more important in the investigation of the former, archaeology, for example; while some are only applicable to the latter, dialogue with those contemporarily Expressing the faiths in question falling into this category: and

(ii) there is greater likelihood of link-up with contemporary problems and issues, for example political and philosophical ones, when one deals with the living.

Third, a large number of religions, for rather accidental reasons, have tended to be treated separately from the world religions and the dead religions, namely those which have come within the purview of social anthropology (itself really a branch of sociology) [9]. These have been somewhat segregated and made into the speciality of anthropology, though there is no special logic in this arrangement beyond the fact that special techniques need to be used in the description of such things as tribal societies. These religions themselves have long histories (hard to penetrate however), are widely divergent, and are mostly living.

The inventory of religions forms the basis of the spectrum of *histories* of religion which is one major aspect of Religion. In so far as these histories attempt to bring out the structures of religions descriptively, they will incorporate the dynamic structural presentation referred to earlier. We might say that the activity of the explorer of a religion in the first instance is the *historical phenomenology* of that religion. So far, religions with no historical overlap could be treated quite independently (for example, ancient Egyptian religion and the religion of the Ainu). In this sense the history of religions is very much *histories* of religions.

It may be noted in passing that the term 'history of religions' is often used, for example, by the International Association for the History of Religions, to refer to, roughly, what I here call Religion. The title, though, implies a certain emphasis upon history and also that there is something like a common method. This last point is correct, and its force could be brought out by saying that there are common tools for studying the histories of religions. It is also desirable that some standardisation of categories for describing religions historically should be attained, provided it is not taken so far as to distort. The reason for this is that it paves the way for asking whether there are recurrent patterns in groups of religions, whether there is *per contra* something very special about a particular religion, and so on. These questions are relevant to the

40

attempt to frame structural explanations, both in sociology and psychology and in Religion itself (this is a provisional way of putting the matter, as we shall see, for strictly psychology of religion and sociology of religion belong to Religion as well as to sociology and psychology).

The elaboration of a standardised set of categories, of types of religious items, is the task of *typological phenomenology*, necessarily comparative in its approach (10). A notable example of this is G. van der Leeuw's 'Religion in Essence and Manifestation' [11]. Not all the categories may be acceptable – typological phenomenology must of course be revisionary in its approach (for example, consider terms like 'monism', 'pantheism', 'polytheism', 'dualism', all used in connection with various religious systems often loosely and frequently in need of refinement. The facts that phenomenologists have tended to start from Western presuppositions and a Western vocabulary have not always helped [12]. The very organic nature of a religion [13], so that one item is affected in its meaning by the rest of the structure, means that typology is a delicate task.

Quite often what is meant by 'comparative study of religion' is typological phenomenology. Consider Rudolf Otto's 'Mysticism East and West [14], comparing the teachings and mysticism of Eckhart and Śankara. But so many pursuits have tended to come under the title – Theology of other religions, missiology, dialogue both exploratory and Theological – that it is wise to abandon the phrase. Further, it has tended to be shorthand for the study of religions other than Christianity, and this is not a rational way to carve up Religion.

So far, then, we have two main activities of religion: histories of religion, including historical phenomenology; and typological phenomenology of religion. Their results can be debatable, but their intention is descriptive and presentational (including bracketed Expression), not Expressive. Though important pursuits in their own right, as bringing out the history and meaning of a variety of religions, they also prepare the way for speculation, for the materials produced are liable to be *suggestive* of patterns of explanation of a structural kind. These, crudely, can be of two sorts (and their mixture), namely explanations which are internal to religion and those which are

41

external. To explain this I must at last embark, at least sketchily, upon the attempt at a definition or characterisation of religion. In doing this I am attempting to bring out some typical elements or *dimensions* as I shall call them of religious traditions. There are other things to say, which I leave aside here, about what it means to say that someone is a religious person.

A religious tradition consists in the first place of people organised institutionally, where the institutions are either specifically and separately devoted to the continuance and Expression of the tradition or where they are not differentiated but form part of the total fabric of a society (even here, however, there will be religious *specialism*, the role of the shaman being a typical example). We may call this the social dimension of a religion.

The activities of the people of a religious tradition will incorporate centrally (so far as the people are concerned with *religion*) rituals, that is, prayers, worship, offerings, festivals, ascetic practices, etc. Even those groups with anti-ritualistic bias have rituals; for example, the Society of Friends continues a certain pattern of meetings. One can have rituals without being ritualistic: briefly, this means that less efficacy and importance is attached to recurrent forms of religious activity than to (say) inner experience, or good works, or right belief, etc. I shall call this the *ritual* dimension of religion.

Though the term 'experience' is a slippery and loose one, it is not unreasonable to point to types of experiences which accompany rituals or which may arise otherwise in the religious context. Some are dramatic and highly formative of religious history, such as the conversion of Paul, the call of Muhammad, the Enlightenment of the Buddha; others are 'humbler', more fragmentary, but nevertheless important for the feel and impact of faith and ritual, some of these being explored in Otto's 'The Idea of the Holy' to mention but one prime instance of the typological phenomenology of religious experience. I refer to all this, somewhat abstractly, as the *experiential* dimension of a religious tradition.

But the institutions nurturing the rituals and the experiences are necessarily interpreted in a certain direction. The prayers

42

are addressed in a certain way, for instance, and thus they cannot be understood save through the intentions of the participants. These themselves involve beliefs of various kinds, which somewhat formally can be categorised into the doctrinal, the mythic, and the ethical. By doctrinal beliefs, I refer to those which say what the structure of this world and the other world is like – the existence and nature of God, gods, spirits; the nature of nirvana; the impermanence of things, and so on. By mythic beliefs I mean those which concern the moving histories of the transcendental entities, etc. – the story of the origin of things; the history of the saviour; the unfolding of the future; the birth and death of evil; the encounters of gods and men. Within this category I would include the story of Christ, that is, I do not treat the mythic as historically false, for the mythic belief may or may not be anchored to history. These dimensions, then, I call the *doctrinal* and the *mythic* respectively. Finally, the *ethical* dimension is constituted by the moral and social beliefs of a tradition (or of a 'section' of a tradition).

Needless to say these distinctions are crude and they need to be viewed under the organic aspect of a religion. The doctrinal beliefs hook up with myths, and in turn hook up with the ethical; all these in turn relate to the ritual, experiential, and institutional life of the tradition. There is a multifarious logic relating the dimensions into which I shall not at the moment enter.

Also there are untidinesses. What of religious art and music? What of symbolism? I treat the former as material adjuncts of or expressions of ritual at the one end, myth and doctrine at the other. I treat the latter as a form under which doctrine and myth are presented. Despite the crudity and untidiness, however, the six-dimensional account of a religious tradition can help to develop what I mean by the other crude distinction I presented, namely that between external and internal explanations.

An internal explanation typically involves trying to show the explanatory connection of an item or items in one dimension with an item or items in another dimension. For example, the myth and ritual school were keen to show how the significance

43

of myths could be illuminated and in part explained by the ritual setting in which the myths were re-enacted. Again it is possible to indicate correlations between the phenomenology of religious experiences and the devotional, contemplative, and other patterns of ritual activity in religions. Likewise, some mystical doctrines (for instance) have at least a partial explanation in the type of experience of the mystic [15].

External explanations, on the other hand, try to show how religious items are shaped by structures not in themselves falling wholly within the territory marked out by the definition of religion. For instance, the shape of a particular myth may be in part determined by the exigencies of the kinship-system in the society in which it is recited. More sweepingly, the dominance of mother-goddesses in certain phases of religions might be at least partially ascribed to the emergence of agriculture. Conversely, some features of a society may be heavily influenced by religion itself, in which case the direction of the explanation runs the other way. Naturally, there can also be a mutual dynamic – a dialectic in which a religion and its society help to shape one another.

For these reasons it is unrealistic for Religion simply to treat of religions in themselves: it necessarily engages with what we may dub 'dialectical' studies, that is, those where there are external explanations, typically tending to run in both directions. Such dialectical studies are: sociology of religion, psychology of religion, history of ideas, history of art, of music, etc. and Literature. But this list cross-classifies to some extent, since history of ideas overlaps with sociology of knowledge; while the study of literature may in part have to do with history of ideas and in part with symbolism analogous to that exhibited in art and even in music. Let us lump together the study of religious art, music, poetry, and so forth, as symbology, a study arising from the products of myth and ritual. We might then set forth the major constituents of Religion, relevantly to our earlier characterisation of the dimensions of religion and to the distinction between typological phenomenology and history, as follows.

Since there are a large number of religions, listed in the inventory, there are many histories. I shall here refer to just two examples; the history of Christianity and the history of Buddhism. In accordance with the division of religion into six dimensions, plus their symbolic products (art, etc.), it is possible to study the history of a religion aspectually (concentrating on one dimension or division of dimensions) or holistically, while dialectical studies themselves may be chiefly historical or chiefly structural. I shall set the various possibilities out in sequence.

Characterisation of religion
1. Belief division: (a) doctrines; (b) myths; (c) ethical and social beliefs.
2. Practical manifestations division: (d) rituals and practices; (e) experiences and sentiments; (f) institutions; (g) symbolism: art, music, poetry as products primarily of (b) and (d).

I. Histories of religions: (A) Christianity; (B) Buddhism; etc.
  (i) holistic; history of Christianity; history of Buddhism.
  (ii) divisional
      (1) beliefs; history of Christian doctrine, etc.; history of Buddhist doctrine, etc.
      (2) practical manifestations; not usually separated out from holistic histories.
  (iii) aspectual; (a), (b), and (c) usually treated together (but see below under 'itemised histories').
      (d) rituals; history of Christian worship; history of Buddhist Yoga, rituals, etc.
      (e) experiences; descriptive psychology of Christianity through the ages; descriptive psychology of Buddhism through the ages.
      (f) institutions; history of Christian institutions; history of Buddhist institutions.
      (g) symbolism; history of Christian art, etc.; history of Buddhist art, etc.
  (iv) itemised histories, that is, the selection of a particular item to treat historically. *Examples*:
      (a) doctrines; history of the doctrine of Creation; development of the doctrine of impermanence.

(b) myths; history of apocalyptic; history of belief in Mara.

(c) ethical beliefs; history of Christian attitudes to war; history of doctrine of non-violence.

(d) rituals; history of the Eucharist; history of Buddhist cult of relics.

(e) experiences; history of Western mysticism; history of Buddhist *bhakti*.

(f) institutions; history of episcopacy; history of Sangha in Ceylon.

(g) symbolism; history of iconography of the Transfiguration; history of *mudras* in Buddhist sculpture.

II. Historical–dialectical studies:
  (i) holistic; Western social history; Eastern social history.
  (ii) divisional:
    (1) beliefs; history of ideas (Western, etc.); history of ideas (Indian, etc.).
    (2) practical manifestations; usually treated aspectually rather than divisionally.
  (iii) aspectual; (a), (b), and (c) usually treated divisionally (see above).
    (d, g, f) rituals and symbolism; history of art, etc. (Western, etc.); history of Indian, etc., art, etc.
    (e) experiences; not usually dealt with separately.
  (iv) itemised histories. *Examples*:
    (a) doctrines; study of the influence of Hegelianism on nineteenth-century Christian theology; history of Indian linguistics and its bearing on Buddhist views of language.
    (b) myths; study of the interpretation of *Genesis* in the light of the evolutionary debate in the mid-nineteenth century; the study of the development of Indian astronomy.
    (c) ethical beliefs; study of the Protestant ethic and the growth of capitalism; history of use of drugs in early India.
    (d, g, f) rituals and symbolism; study of humanist values in religious art in the Renaissance; study

of Indian trade-routes in relation to patterns of Buddhist pilgrimage.

III. Phenomenological and structural studies:
- (i) structural description; presentation of structure of Christianity in a given social milieu at a given time; presentation of Buddhism in a given milieu at a given time.
- (ii) typological phenomenology (general); for example, an inventory of types of religious items, as in van der Leeuw, 'Religion in Essence and Manifestation'.
- (iii) typological phenomenology (general, but aspectual):
  - (a) doctrines; comparative theology.
  - (b) myths; comparative mythics.
  - (c) ethics; comparative ethics.
  - (d) rituals; comparative practics (but frequently such terms as 'worship' may be used, though not fully comprehensive – cp. Geoffrey Parrinder, 'Worship in the World's Religions').
  - (e) experiences; comparative descriptive psychology of religion.
  - (f) institutions; comparative sociology of religion (descriptive).
- (iv) typological phenomenology (itemised). *Examples*:
  - (a) doctrines; comparison of the doctrines of Nagarjuna and Mansel.
  - (b) myths; comparison of figures of Satan and Mara.
  - (c) ethics; comparison of Buddhist and Christian attitudes to war.
  - (d) rituals; comparison of Buddhist and Christian contemplative techniques.
  - (e) experiences; comparison of Christian and Buddhist mystical experiences.
  - (f) institutions; comparison of roles of priesthood in Catholicism and Tibetan Buddhism.
  - (g) symbolism; study of mandalas and analogous representations in the Christian tradition.
- (v) internal structural explanations. *Examples*:

47

explanation of the Buddhist *trikaya* doctrine in relation to growth of *bhakti* alongside Buddhist yoga, etc.;

explanation of doctrine of incomprehensibility of God as expression of sentiment of awe;

correlation between doctrines of grace and experiences of a devotional–numinous type.

IV. Dialectical–phenomenological studies:
   (i) sociology of religion and anthropology of religion (general).
   (ii) aspectual, for example structural anthropology as applied to myth; sociology of knowledge.
   (iii) psychology of religion (general).
   (iv) aspectual, for example the psychology of religious symbolism.
   (v) itemised studies within these fields.
   (vi) philosophy of religion, in so far as it may be concerned with conceptual and methodological problems arising in and out of dialectical-phenomenological studies (for example problems about sociological uses of the concept of rationality in the context of the study of religion).

This so far is a pretty full inventory of the activities which may be said to fall within the scope of Religion. It may be noted that the process of dialogue, in so far as it is only concerned with mutual understanding (and does not progress to a form of mutual theologising), is an important technique in what I have dubbed typological phenomenology. It may also be noted that phenomenology as a structural description of a particular religion at t_1 is a slice, so to say, out of a holistic history of that religion. Where there is a succession of structural slices, one has the dynamic moving picture of a faith to which I referred earlier. That is, a deep history involves phenomenological presentation.

We may now return to one of the questions posed by the quotation from Eliade. Is there something over and above the activities listed above, which is a special task of Religion, namely the practice of a creative hermeneutics?

It seems in a way inevitable, for reasons which I shall outline

48

shortly, but first a warning must be issued. If religion is to be studied as a phenomenon, as for instance we might study political behaviour, it is essential to distinguish, as we have done, between Religion and Theologies. It would be most unfortunate if the slogan of a creative hermeneutics itself paved the way for a secret Theologising and a betrayal of the spirit of sympathetic objectivity. And I scarcely need to repeat that a subject or field (e.g., Religion) should not be defined from a position *within* it. This warning against an uncandidness, a failure to bring presuppositions out into the light of conscious awareness, is necessary if we are to see the creative hermeneutic in its true perspective.

The reasons for supposing that Eliade is in a way right, though they do not necessarily correspond to *his* reasons, are as follows. First, part of the task of Religion is, of course, interpreting religions, through bracketed Expression, to use the jargon which I have been employing here. Now we need to consider: for whom is a religion being interpreted? We have hinted already that in different countries there will in all likelihood be different rates of investment of effort in presenting religions, for there will be a case for giving some extra priority to the religion or religions of a given cultural tradition in which the task of interpretation is taking place. Nevertheless, in principle one needs to construct a worldwide constituency of those for whom religions are being interpreted. And certainly it is not the case that the clientele here are committed to a given faith. The constituency is thus much, much wider than that to which a given Theology is in the first instance directed (to bring about a self-understanding of the tradition or faith which the Theology is designed to express). This fact means that Religion, if it is successful, will introduce a sympathetically objective awareness of religious pluralism. This is not at all to say that it introduces a pluralistic Theology, like that of Radhakrishnan (seeing a kind of unity in the varieties of religious tradition – a pluralism-in-unity) [16]. But if successful it inevitably creates an internalised consciousness of the richness of human attitudes, symbols, beliefs. This is itself liable to raise the question of what humanity in this new cultural posture towards religions is to make of them. It would be artificial for the Religionist to

49

present the meanings of faiths and cultures and then simply to contract out of the question of their significance in the larger perspective of human history and a new global humanity.

Second, the pursuit of Religion does, after all, express a type of specialism, admittedly a very rich and broadly-based one. Thus a training in Religion can give some licence to pronounce with some expertise and sensitivity on the place of religions in human history and on the seeds of possible future developments.

However, it must be recognised that the task of a creative hermeneutics, as envisaged by Eliade, is necessarily very *speculative*. In trying to develop ideas on the significance or meaning of religion (and religions) in human history and especially during the present cultural epoch, when something of a world cultural community is in process of being created, the Religionist can hope for no trans-Theological orthodoxy. Consider, for instance, the ambiguity of 'significance':

(i) The understanding of a diversity of religious traditions is a way of understanding their significance, i.e., what they mean to those who belong to these traditions, both in the past and at the present time.

(ii) Certain values in a religious tradition may be significant to us because they throw light upon ethical and social problems at present besetting us.

(iii) Religious traditions may be significant because they contain materials for Expressing the truth about the world and about human life.

(iv) The significance of religion might be viewed in terms of the role it has played in human society, art, etc.

(v) The significance of religion may have to be seen in the light of the most plausible and sensitive theories of its *genesis*: for instance, does the myth-making aspect of human culture throw light on the structure of human social psychology? or again: are religious beliefs a form of projection, and if so, is such projection inescapable?

These and other overlapping senses of 'significance' and 'meaning' throw light on the ambiguities contained in the very notion of a creative hermeneutics. And in any case we here tangle, almost inevitably, with rival Theologies. In reflecting thus on the results of Religion we spiral backwards into the league of religious Expressions which we undertook to study and present from a higher, bracketing standpoint.

Perhaps an analogy can be made with the history and philosophy of science. To do philosophy of science it is necessary to be acquainted with the practice of science; and a grounding in the history of this is also of the greatest importance if the philosophising is to remain realistic and not absurdly *a priori*. Moreover, the history of science can often be so suggestive for the evolution of ideas about its methodology, etc. However, it can sometimes happen that a scientific revolution itself has reflexive elements, that is, it arises from philosophical considerations about the nature of science or of some particular concepts currently in use. Thus Einstein's Theory of Relativity was in part born out of reflection upon fundamental concepts. A philosophy of science is implicit in the interpretation of quantum mechanics in the work of the Copenhagen school. This reflexivity has its parallel in Religion, for not merely does Religion have reflective effects within Theology, say Christian Theology, but also Religion, having completed its primary tasks of history and phenomenology, is liable to become involved in philosophical and speculative questions on the borders between sociology, psychology, phenomenology, and Theologies. It cannot be wrong for the Religionist to comment or even to try his hand at some kind of synthesis, provided he recognises with full clarity that he is here entering the realm of speculation and thus is in a way in the same league as religious Expressions. If this is what is meant by creative hermeneutics, then the enterprise is an epiphenomenon, so to say, of Religion; but it should not corrupt the Religionist into a dogmatic slanting of the evidence and the meanings which the main body of his discipline so painstakingly needs to present.

Unfortunately, nothing very precise can be said about the possibilities of the varied expressions of creative hermeneutics, though shadowy examples can be provided; for example, the attempt to interpret religious traditions as expressing what can otherwise be put Existentially (a generalised version of the enterprise of Rudolf Bultmann); or the attempt at a Marxist interpretation. My view is that these particular, if shadowy projects, are scarcely likely to succeed in the face of the evidence, any more than that of Freudian or of Jungian psychology to interpret religion for modern men. I say this because of the nature of these interpretations and of the state of the evidence provided by Religion [17]. It is not easy to predict the future of a line of enquiry. Future methods and concepts so often transcend present methods and concepts. So in brief the project of Eliade is not absurd; however, it does not entail a single hermeneutic for Religion (but a variety of debatable ones); it is an epiphenomenon of the main substance of Religion, and it is unpredictable. But we can be sure that no total picture of the nature of man can be complete unless it contains a theory of religion.

The main argument of this chapter has been concerned with trying to exhibit religion and religions through uncovering the anatomy of Religion. I have also introduced a strong distinction between Theologies on the one hand and Religion on the other, even if it has been modified somewhat in the course of discussion. This modification has been achieved mainly through the notion that Expression can be bracketed, so that Religion itself exhibits, but without *directly* Expressing, what it is that the Expresser is attempting to convey. Despite the obliqueness of the major way of characterising religions, I have also adopted the more direct approach of considering religious traditions under a number of dimensions or aspects. This has helped in the anatomising of Religion.

Among a number of crudities left unrefined has been the occasional reference to religion as phenomenon (items of religions as phenomena); since it is often a slogan to say that the scientific study, Religion, is directed at religion as a phenomenon, a slogan important in what it is trying to exclude, namely Theology, I shall turn in the second chapter to a closer examination of this idea.

2 Religion as a Phenomenon

In part, talk of religion as a phenomenon has sprung from the tradition of philosophical phenomenology (from Husserl onwards), whose methods, with variations, have been applied to the study of religion. In part my approach in the previous chapter has been influenced by this school, for example in the notion of 'bracketing'. Gerardus van der Leeuw, in an appendix to his 'Religion in Essence and Manifestation, [1], has characterised phenomenological method as follows: (i) assigning names to what is manifested (e.g., 'sacrifice' and 'purification'); (ii) the interpolation of the phenomenon into our own lives, sympathetically; (iii) the application of *epoche*; (iv) the clarification of what is observed, by structural association (comparison and contrast); (v) the achievement through the foregoing of understanding; (vi) control and checking by philology, archaeology, etc.; (vii) the realisation of objectivity, or in other words letting the facts speak for themselves.

It will be observed that Gerardus van der Leeuw's programme here falls chiefly under the head of descriptive, structural studies (phenomenology and typological phenomenology). and does not seriously touch upon psychology and sociology of religion as involved in structural *explanations*. But a central part in Religion will obviously be taken by descriptive phenomenology, roughly as he envisages it, which provides importantly the material which structural explanations will work with. However, the concept of religious phenomena is not a simple one and needs unravelling.

Let us consider a particular example. What precisely would it involve if the Anglican Eucharist were treated, by this method, as a 'phenomenon'? I choose this example partly because of its relative familiarity to many readers, partly to short-circuit problems about archaeology, etc. (clearly the problems of phenomenology are multiplied by distance in time).

53

First, we may notice that 'the Anglican Eucharist' is a notion somewhat like 'symphony'. The same symphony, as we say, is played on a variety of occasions (this is like the type-token distinction sometimes made use of in philosophical linguistics). To distinguished between the idea of the same Eucharist enacted on different occasions, I shall speak respectively of *the* Eucharist and *a* Eucharist. To complicate matters, there are variations in *the* Eucharist – differing forms under which it is enacted. Where such divergences are relevant we speak of *the Eucharists*.

Second, we can begin to unravel the complexities of what it means to speak of the Eucharist as a phenomenon by considering what an obesrver or set of observers might be held to see by attending Eucharists. Crudely, and superficially, they see a group of people performing certain actions with certain instruments in a certain sort of building (typically). Already we note that even at this superficial level they are liable to have to collect their impressions of what is typical of the type. Not all Eucharists take place in churches, and some may exotically make use of tea and leavened bread rather than wine and unleavened wafers [2]. To be complete the observers could in principle describe the whole spectrum of external objects and observances. However, what the observers 'observe' in this superficial manner does not bring out at all adequately that the 'phenomenon' is, for it is at least a human phenomenon (whether it is wholly so we need to consider later), and to understand what an action is one has to understand something about its intentionality. Thus, for example, seeing someone kneeling is not just someone with his legs bent in a certain way: one is seeing someone bending his legs in a certain way and intending his being in that posture as a case of kneeling. In that sense, some one shot in the knees who slumps to a kneeling posture is not really kneeling. We can say: 'He ended up in a kneeling position' but it would be a trifle misleading to say 'He is kneeling'. Further, someone kneeling in church is not merely intending his posture as kneeling; but is also intending his kneeling as part of what is involved in prayer and worship; for one can kneel for other reasons than sacred ones.

The observers therefore need to understand a framework of intentions, and indeed it is artificial to say that they do not

54

observe people kneeling and praying (provided they have these concepts, which surely are part of the common stock of most peoples. But of course often we may encounter concepts important for the understanding of intentions which have rather subtly to be learned and this is an important hazard in the delicacies of the phenomenology of religion). At any rate, we may deem our observers to have at least got to the stage of perceiving a group of people engaged in certain activities such as praying. What more do they have to perceive to perceive the phenomenon of a Eucharist?

One thing they have to recognize is that the activity is a communal one, not just a coincidence of individual actions. Not all religious actions have this communal character, but it is fair to say that communality is a central feature of religions, such that even individual actions will be somehow related to them – the monk contemplating in his cell is part of a movement with shared ideals and practices. The communality of a Eucharist is brought out not merely by the fact that the people do roughly the same things at the same times (for example, recite the Lord's Prayer at the same time) but more deeply by the fact that they conceive their actions as joint. A person praying conceives himself not merely to be individually praying to God, but as joining with others in a collective prayer to God. So far the phenomenon involves: 'external' events and instruments; actions categorised as, for example, praying; a communality of actions.

The communality, however, is not just a communality of those present at a Eucharist, or a set of communalities of a set of groups at Eucharist. The observers have to see more deeply into the intentions of the participants. Relevantly, they have to see that a group at a Eucharist conceives itself as participating in a Eucharist, that is, that this Eucharist is an enactment of *the* Eucharist. So the group in performing this set of actions expresses a wider communality, one extending at least as widely as their Church.

But here already the phenomenon is casting very wide conceptual and institutional tendrils. The phenomenon as a particular item is systematically connected with a scheme of belief and an institutional tradition. Here is an instance of the organic

55

character of a religion [3] and of the methodological inadequacy of treating items in isolation. The phenomenon is turning into a very complex one. However, let us return to the immediate group at a Eucharist.

The observers, in seeing certain actions as prayers, may have a general understanding of what is going on, for they understand what prayer is. But to grasp the fine grain of the 'phenomenon', they need to understand the particularities of the prayers, not of course just their words, but the nature of the Focus at which they are directed. It is here that a serious set of complications sets in; complications partly touched upon in the previous chapter but about which we must achieve as much clarity as possible. They are incidentally, relevant to the question of whether religion can be treated by Religion as a purely human 'phenomenon'.

The persons participating in a Eucharist will typically conceive that the Focus is in a special way present to them; for instance, the bread and wine somehow are or become the body and blood of Christ. Further, the circumstances of the communal act will suggest that God is among them in a different way from that in which he is present always and everywhere to those who turn to him individually in prayer. At any rate, part of what is involved in a Eucharist is the addressing of the Focus and the sense of participation in the Focus, through the act of communion. Is the Focus therefore part of the phenomenon which the observers witness? Is what they see an interplay between the Focus and human acts, such as prayer? In a way, yes; but we need to be careful about what is meant by this.

First, there is the problem of bracketing. Is the observer committed to the existence of the Focus? The notion that phenomenology 'brackets' questions of Theological truth would imply not. Yet at first sight much would seem to turn on the presuppositions to be adopted in any description of the Eucharist. Consider some more empirical 'common-sensical' assumptions that an observer present at a Eucharist might make: for instance he is able to say that the gold mosaic behind the altar channels the attention of the worshippers upon the crucifix standing silhouetted by it; or that the central position of the pulpit tends to emphasise the importance of preaching as part

56

of the rite. Here the observer is talking about the impact of the arrangements upon the participant, but the arrangements are material and not precisely in dispute. There is no question about the existence of the mosaic, the crucifix, and the pulpit; no question either about the bread and the wine. Now admittedly the observer may not accept the real existence of the Focus, but from the point-of-view of the experience, sentiments, and actions of the participants there is no special reason to doubt the importance of the impact of the Focus: this could be greater than any material impact, like the effects of gazing at the mosaic and the crucifix or listening to the words of a centrally-placed preacher (though here incidentally one must watch the question of whether the preaching itself is not also a sacrament, Expressing the Focus which is thereby present in it).

We might arrive at an over-simple solution of the problem by saying that the observers, *qua* observers, are simply not in a position to affirm the Focus, without bracketing, for it is the prerogative of those who have faith to affirm the Focus. But is it enough for the observers to say that the Focus, though 'real' to the participants, is not 'real' to the observers? For after all, the observers need to *describe* the situation, and it might (it would be thought) make a difference as to what items are included as real factors in the situation. Suppose, again, that the observers are in fact Christians: why then should they be precluded in describing the Focus with as much realism as they reserve for the mosaic and the preaching?

One of the problems revealed by these questions is that descriptions are not just what they seem to be but that they contain explanations or at least incipient explanations. In particular they tend to imply explanations relevant to mental causation. For example, I am walking along a lane in Italy and suddenly stop, my heart beating, at the sight of a viper. The description that might be given, 'He was frightened by a viper on the way to San Martino', is apt enough, and assumes the existence of a snake. It would scarcely be right just to say, ' Firmly believing it was a snake in the way, he was scared'. That already begins to imply that there was no snake. On the other hand, it can make no difference, from my point-of-view, whether the snake is real or not, provided that I am sure it is a snake. Suppose I am walking home in the dusk and mistake a coiled rope for a snake. I still stop, my heart still starts pounding, and yet a describer might want to say: 'Mistaking a coil of rope for a snake, he stopped, his heart pounding.' Two main features of the descriptive situation may be noted here. First, a description tries, so to say, to comment on the true state of affairs (whether there was a snake or not); and second, it tends to have an explanatory air (since snakes, for example, are typically fear-inducing, so that one can understand why a coil of rope causes fear, provided that one knows that it has been mistaken for a snake: consider how the above descriptions would work if we substituted 'coil of rope' for 'snake' and conversely!). Both these features of descriptions run into a certain amount of trouble when we try to apply them to phenomenological description in Religion.

First, from what point-of view is the phenomenological description going to comment on the 'true state of affairs'? The analogy of the coil of rope and the snake does not quite work, since this analogy depends upon fairly clear criteria of what counts as a snake, how one identifies a snake, and opposedly how one identifies a coil of rope. These conditions are not met in regard to determining whether there is or is not a Focus present at the Eucharist and what nature that Focus has. There are not, in plainer words, clear criteria for establishing the existence or non-existence of God. Therefore secondly there are equally severe doubts about the acceptability of any explanatory suggestions contained in a description of the state of affairs at the Eucharist.

It is easy to think that these problems can be escaped by reducing the description of the Eucharist to that of a purely human phenomenon. That is, it is tempting to suppose that the Focus can be interpreted 'scientifically' as a human projection of some kind. Then the account of the Eucharist simply refers to the interplay between this projected Focus and the actions of the participants. A path of this kind is trodden by Peter Berger in his 'The Social Reality of Religion' [4], though here he is not primarily concerned with phenomenology but with the sociology of religion. He espouses what he calls 'methodological atheism' (pp. 100 and 180), a term derived from Anton Zijderveld. 'The essential perspective,' he writes (p. 180), 'of the socio-

58

logical theory here proposed is that religion is to be understood as a human projection, grounded in specific infrastructures of human history.' He of course distinguishes this methodological atheism from atheism *tout court*. But one needs to ask what it is in the way of explanations that is excluded by methodological atheism. And further, is it merely a device for operating within 'scientific' sociology? If this be so, then is it assumed that a total account or explanation of religion can be given from a sociological point-of-view? The last is a very bold assumption, but less extravagant perhaps when one realises that sociological theory tends to subsume other spheres of human enquiry such as psychology within its embrace. Even so, it is an assumption which will need examining in due course. Meanwhile, let us examine the projectionist account of the Focus.

It should be noted first that the language of projection encapsulates a theory of the genesis of religion. Religion is here conceived as essentially a human product, though objectivated, so that it appears to have a being of its own and also in a certain way has an independent dynamic, like other products of human culture such as language. Although Berger leaves open the possibility that there is no incompatibility between Theology and methodological atheism (even if some Theologies may be called in question by sociology), it is not certain how this will help us in regard to the problems posed in phenomenological description. For if phenomenology is to be assimilated into its brother sociology, then it also ought to proceed with a methodological atheism — but already this is to suggest that a certain kind of description has to be given of, for example, the Eucharist, a description, that is, which comments on the 'true state of affairs'. Such a comment would include reference, presumably, to the projected character of the Focus. At this juncture methodological atheism would be effectively indistinguishable from atheism *tout court*. Yet one of the major problems about phenomenological description is that raised by the difficulty in finding *clear* criteria of what is or is not 'there', what is existent as a Focus of the activities of the participants in the Eucharist. Still the fact that methodological atheism tries to remain merely methodological is a point in its favour if one is trying seriously to operate the *epoche* and the neutral, but evocative 'bracketing' which

59

seems to be demanded by the pursuit of phenomenology in the context of Religion.

Suppose we were to veer to the other extreme, and instead of treating the Focus itself as an objectivated human product, to say *tout court* that God in Christ is present in the Eucharist. The Theologian and the faithful might applaud; after all this is for them a true description of the state of affairs. And by the very fact that the criteria of truth are obscure, there can be no disproof that this description is not the right one. But there are obvious difficulties in taking this extreme. Does it imply (on the sauce-for-the-goose-sauce-for-the-gander principle) that one should also give a 'realistic', reality-affirming description of the rites of the Kikuyu and the Vaishnavite, the Taoist and the Winnebago? Let us suppose it does.

Then the ontological firmament becomes heavily populated, and rather inconsistently. Let us conceive one Focus to be a jealous God; then how can he be affirmed in description side-by-side with many gods? In serving many masters the phenomenologist is liable to betray man, so that his 'realism' is scarcely any advantage. He may try out an uneasy half-way house, the many Foci have something essential shared between them; for example, they are all 'manifestations' of the Holy. He may not in one way be unjustified in this, for part at least of his task is to categorise, to seek out common features as well as to exhibit divergencies. Indeed the seeking out of common features is prominent in the Husserlian tradition, which includes the search for 'essences'. But in trying now to describe the Eucharist 'realistically' he loses the very particularity, the fine grain, which he was seeking to grasp in giving a refined and sensitive description of it. The realistic extreme then has collapsed into an indefinite state, but scarcely one which can function effectively as a *via media* between projection and fine-grained realism.

It may be recalled that the problem of phenomenological description partly arose from the features of description – its tendency to comment on the true state of affairs and to hint at explanations. But whereas in the case of snakes and coils of rope there can be a definite and agreed state of affairs, this is not so with regard to theism, atheism, Christianity, Buddhism, etc. In this the cases are not parallel and there can be no necessity

60

for the phenomenologist to rush into necessarily debatable 'realistic' descriptions or to incorporate theories of religion into his account. Indeed it is very important, precisely because of the debatability of the issues, *not* to load descriptions with explanatory theories (for example, by the use of the expression 'projection'); for although it would be naive to suppose that by waiting till all the facts are gathered we can ultimately resolve the issues of explanation and so forth, it is nevertheless profoundly true that the theories have to be tested by reference to the facts. These facts include intentional ones: they are facts of consciousness, so to speak, as well as directly observable ones. But when facts become over-contaminated by theory, theory itself loses its golden falsifiability and its golden verifiability, thereby ceasing to be properly scientific. Thus even from the point-of-view of those who might at first sight veer towards the side of methodological atheism, it is important to resist it.

The difference over criteria may also help to explain why the procedure of bracketing is more natural regarding religion and ideologies than it is if systematically applied to much of the rest of experience. It is somewhat unnatural to say such things as 'He had an experience as of a snake', *except* when actually it is something other than a snake that he sees, because the criteria allow us indisputable paradigms of seeing actual snakes. To bracket is to leave matters too open as to whether these are after all paradigms.

The upshot of this discussion would seem to lie in the acceptance of a bracketed realism in the description of phenomena, such as a Eucharist. One aspect of what is meant by bracketing could be brought out by saying that an entity referred to in brackets might or might not exist. For instance, at a Eucharist people pray to Christ and he is present in the bread and wine (but he might or might not exist). This account of bracketing, however, suffers from at least two defects. First and less importantly, the sentence 'He might or might not exist' appears to be an utterance on a par with the utterances of the Christian. This of course will not do at all, for as a straight religious or quasi-religious utterance the sentence in question is liable to express indifference, agnosticism, or the like. But the phenomenologist (and more generally the Religionist) is not *qua* phenomenologist

61

(or Religionist) committed to indifference, agnosticism, or what have you, any more than he is thereby committed to Christianity, Buddhism, or the religion of the Kikuyu or of the Winnebago. So 'He might or might not exist' is a bad way of saying 'The question of his existence does not arise in this methodological framework'. It is a question not asked, not a question left undecided. True, it might be asked later, once the work of pure phenomenology is done, but that is another story. The second defect of the above account of bracketing is this.

The account does not yet give us a guide as to which entities and events are to be bracketed and which are not. For example, it is not right to bracket the claim that people are praying. It is simply the case that they are praying, if they are praying, whatever we may think of the Focus of their prayers. An initial distinction might be as follows: that what belongs to the doctrinal, mythic and ethical dimensions of religion needs bracketing, while the rest does not. But this distinction scarcely works and for a number of reasons. First, an experience (like Paul's conversion on the Damascus Road) is already 'interpreted', so do we accept the experience and bracket the interpretation? Up to a point this seems a sound procedure, but what is the point at which we change the mode of description? Second, a ritual object means something to the person who uses it over and above the doctrinal ambience in which it has its being. Third, something observable and concrete, such as an historical event or series of events, may need, in its way, bracketing. So if someone speaks of the Hungarian counter-revolution (referring to the events of 1956), the term 'counter-revolution' needs bracketing, for it trails clouds of orthodox ideology with it. Still, despite these objections, the rough distinction is serviceable, though it needs further explication.

The doctrinal, mythic, and (less so) ethical dimensions of a religious tradition are the means whereby that religious tradition Expresses its faith in the Focus (or group of Foci) of the tradition. Thus these dimensions present as it were a picture of the Focus (a piece of terminology introduced in the previous chapter). The Focus itself transcends the doctrines, myths, and so on as it also transcends the practical side of the religion, the rituals, experiences, institutions, symbolic forms, etc. By saying

62

this, I mean that the Focus is what these ideas and practices refer to or are directed at. The faithful have a certain picture or pictures (but we shall here for the time being leave aside the problem of pluralism within a tradition); this picture is Expressed most sophisticatedly in Theology, but also in art and so forth, and it includes an account of the way the Focus *manifests* itself or *is present* in various events, both historical and contemporary. The manifestations of the Focus (I shall use this expression even if strictly the Focus may often manifest itself by non-manifestation, that is by being present in events, even though opaquely – consider the Incarnation or the Eucharist) are typically highly variegated: the historical events, for Christianity, of Christ's life, death and resurrection, the coming of the Holy Spirit in the Early Church, in the institutions of the Church (e.g., the episcopate), in the sacraments, in the experiences, and sentiments of the faithful, even in the actions and experiences of those outside the Church, in the cosmos. Not all these manifestations are accepted as manifestations by all Christians, but the list serves to indicate the breath of the spectrum wherein Christian men see the special presence and handiwork of God. The disagreements, though, are in their way significant. Some agree about the Focus but differ about the scope of the manifestations; some agree about the scope of the manifestations but not about the Focus; some disagree about both; some agree about both. Most typically, there is a conjunction of disagreement about the picture of the Focus and about the manifestations; after all the manifestations are not only the crucial means of *identifying* the Focus but also important elements to be taken into account in delineating the character of the Focus (that is, Expressing a picture of it).

The distinction between manifestation and Focus allows us to refine the solution to the problem of what entities, events, etc., are to be bracketed and what are not. Those which manifest the Focus, and those utterances and so forth which Express the Focus, are to be bracketed so long as they are seen under the categories of manifestation and Expression. For example, the bread and wine at the Eucharists are seen under the aspect of the body and blood of Christ, and so are manifestations of the Focus; the descriptions, etc., of the bread and wine then are bracketed. Again, the 'Our Father, who art in heaven . . .' of the Lord's Prayer is not merely recited at the Eucharist, but treated by the phenomenologist as a bracketed Expression (with descriptive elements) of the faith of those who pray.

However, it would be unrealistic to think that a formula can direct with total effectiveness the job of distinguishing what needs bracketing from what does not. This distinction must in the concrete situation rest upon the sympathetic intuition of the person undertaking the phenomenological enquiry.

There is, however, a further problem for the phenomenologist who uses a bracketed realism in his description of (say) the Eucharist. The hazard is that a word or two may mislead him and his public. For example, the people at the Eucharist pray to a (bracketed) Christ who is present in the celebration. But what Christ? The very use of the name presupposes that we know the reference and understand the nuances in the same way. This is a rather optimistic presupposition. The ambiguities are many and at least as follows.

(i) Christ (hereafter 'the Focus') is the Focus pictured in a particular way by participant A in the celebration; let us call this Focus^A.

(ii) The Focus is the typified Focus of those who participate in the celebration; let us call this Focus^t.

(iii) The Focus is the typified Focus of the wider communality of those to whom the group participating in the celebration affirm themselves to belong; let us call this Focus^T.

(iv) The Focus is the 'real' Focus, transcending the pictures found in the preceding, but recognised in principle by the participants, and by the community at large; let us call this Focus^x.

It will readily be seen that the last Focus is a kind of aspiration (looking at it from the human end); it could in principle be described, but then it would become one of the prior three Foci. On the other hand it is useful as a construct, for it indicates that there may be (or is) a reality which is only inadequately pictured by the present pictures. Indeed, if one were to go beyond a sort of methodological realism and introduce the concept of an ultimate reality impinging, so to say, upon the faithful, and doing so relevantly to problems of explanation in the manner

64

in which descriptions (of snakes and the like) do so, it is probable that it would be Focus^X which would first be thought of. Unfortunately, of course, it is in the nature of the case that this necessary *noumenon* of Foci can have no particular purchase on the world, for it lies beyond particularities and so in an important sense beyond the world of our experience. But a vital question which remains to be answered is: how necessary for the phenomenologist and more widely for the Religionist is this concept of the transcendental Focus^X? To this question we shall in due course return.

Meanwhile, let us reflect on the relations between the other three Foci. It is easy, for example, to think that the whole of the matter is summed up in a collection of Foci^A; that is, to think that a religious tradition essentially is constituted by a collection of individuals who happen to think alike, direct their activities similarly to a similar Focus, and so on. This is not a plausible picture, for a number of reasons. Before we go on to these reasons let us pause for a moment to consider the highly complex task (almost impossibly so) which such a picture of the situation would present to the phenomenologist of religion. Admittedly the latter has a bad task anyway, and necessarily to be completed rather crudely. But it would be well nigh impossible if the observers at a Eucharist did not merely have to take account of 'external' actions but also of the multitude of separate pictures of the Focus, that is, Focus^A, Focus^B, Focus^C, and so on. Now it will immediately be objected that this is the way the world is – men differ, their concepts differ, and so there is no way of representing the total situation but by bringing out these different perspectives in all their richness. And indeed it is hard to deny that men's pictures (individual pictures) of the Focus or Foci *do* differ both subtly and crassly. Does not this make the task of the phenomenologist unbearable, or alternatively his 'results' unbearably crude? Fortunately, though there is truth in the delineation of the actual situation here presented, the situation typically is less individualistic than the picture presented allows. How is this?

First, the Eucharist (for example) cannot be analysed as a construct out of countless individual decisions and experiences almost miraculously tending in the same direction, towards the same Focus, and coinciding in actions. The analysis through individual acts would for one thing be much too coincidental. Second, it has to be recognised that the liturgy of the Eucharist (I am using this as my example, but one could look much more widely on religious institutions, rituals and myths, etc., in the same manner) is 'given', *objectivated* as might be said. It is not the creation of any individual present at a Eucharist; but it is a piece of public or semi-public property, something to be re-enacted from time to time and irrespectively of the particular feelings and acts of an individual. Indeed, the individual, and by extension the individuals, who participate in a Eucharist, *follow* something. This observation does not depend upon any ritualistic understanding of the Eucharist, since similar remarks could be made about a meeting of Friends, *mutatis mutandis*. Third and of course greatly overlapping with what has just been said, the participants see themselves as a community participating in a wider community directed at the same Focus.

Consequently, the phenomenologist is not only concerned with collecting individual impressions. It is reasonable for him to advert to the public meaning of rites and beliefs since in a real sense these are shared. This however does not, as we shall see, altogether exempt him from considering the fine grain of individual responses, and to this extent his results must always be crude, oversimplified, and crass – a property he shares with the historian and the political scientist and many others.

We may conclude then that the phenomenologist is basically concerned with Focus^T and its manifestations, together with the responses, attitudes, etc., of those present at the Eucharist. A description of all *this* will serve to typify the meaning of the Eucharist, in the milieu of Anglicanism. It may turn out to be necessary to show the variations in pictures presented and responses made, as between different 'parties' in the Church of England, and as between Anglican communities in different countries.

It can now be seen why the notion of a noumenal Focus lying, so to speak, beyond Focus^T is in many contexts necessary for the phenomenologist: first, because a noumenal outreach is itself typically built into Focus^T and its analogues in other religions; and second because it expresses the openness and

66

dynamism of a religious tradition. It performs this second task in the following manner. The conception of a noumenal Focus transcending the pictures presented is a regulative device suggesting the construction of new pictures to replace the old. A new picture itself is not noumenal, for the transcendental Focus still serves the same function, namely to suggest that the new picture itself may be replaced.

Why, it may be asked, this emphasis on novelty? It seems a paradox considering the heavily traditional nature of most religions. Certainly the notion of a noumenal Focus or Foci is less relevant in static social and cultural traditions and where there may not be a very consciously developed sense of the picture-transcending nature of the religious ultimate. Nevertheless, the phenomenon of milieu-transformation, bringing about changes of meanings of the 'same' text or rite because of the changes in context, implies a continuous process of adaptation, however conservative; to this extent new pictures are ever liable to be presented, to overcome the changes in milieu-transformation and to achieve as far as possible an equilibrium. The noumenal Focus adverts to this open-endedness. It also creates the space for critical manoeuvre, for instance, space for a prophetic re-presentation of the Focus over against of the traditional pictures.

So far I have largely used the term 'phenomenological description' to indicate the task of our supposed observers of the Eucharist. But as was pointed out in the previous chapter, phenomenology requires also to be evocative, to contain bracketed Expression. What people feel, the impact of the Focus upon them, the performative and expressive nature of the language of worship and prayer, etc. – these are central features of, say, the Eucharist, This is the reason why it is often said that the practice of Religion involves sympathy, so that the Religionist can enter into the 'feel' and the values of the phenomena he is studying.

This is what van der Leeuw refers to as the interpolation of the phenomenon into our own lives. Before, however, going on to consider in a little more detail how such interpolation is possible, it may be useful to pause to consider in the light of the preceding discussion whether it is really apposite to speak of the objects of phenomenological investigations as phenomena, often categorised as *human* phenomena. Let us begin with the second point: in what sense is the phenomenologist concerned merely with human phenomena (beliefs, experiences, etc.)?

We have already rejected projectionism as an assumption in phenomenology itself, partly because it is inconsistent with true bracketing. This is not to exclude it as a theory about religion to be checked against the phenomenological facts. Now if we have rejected projectionism within phenomenology, we cannot hold that phenomenology simply deals with human events and products, though it certainly does at least this. That it does not simply do so might be held on the following grounds.

(i) The phenomenological description of the Eucharist (for example) brings out the interplay, so to speak, between the Focus and the participants. From the point-of-view of phenomenology, the question of whether the Focus exists does not arise; but if it *does* exist, then the phenomenological description does actually describe a manifestation of the Focus, or in other words it is not just a description of human events, etc.

(ii) Phenomenology incorporates into its descriptions non-human entities, for instance sacred cows and planetary bodies. Though a prime point of interest is the way in which humans respond religiously to these entities, and though it might be thought that certain significances are being artificially imposed by human cultures on these entities, even so the 'objective' properties of these entities play some part in determining the religious response. For instance, the urine of the cow is held in India to have purifying powers, but that a cow makes urine is itself a brute non-human fact.

It is thus a simplification to say that Religion concerns human 'phenomena' alone. That we might be tempted to use this language is a reaction against demands that the subject should be Theologically based; for example, starting from the assumption of the truth of a particular faith, mankind is brought in to redress the balance of the other world, so to say. If one turns for a moment to anthropology, one sees here a primary concern with human institutions, but to bring out the pattern of life of a particular people it is necessary to describe their interplay with the environment, and also with their 'supernatural' environment.

68

To speak of human phenomena as being the sole concern of Religion is a simplification, and so too is it to speak of religion as a phenomenon. The phrase is important perhaps as a slogan, to indicate that description and evocation are the prime tasks of phenomenology together with typology, rather than Theological judgements. But the word still trails with it a suggestion that phenomenology deals with appearances: appearances, however, of what? It is not just concerned with how a faith manifests itself or appears in this sense, but rather with how it actually is. Its aim is to give insight and understanding of the substance of men's faiths, the way they actually operate, impinge on institutions, exist in human consciousness and so on. Is it then appearances of the Foci that phenomenology deals with? But this is a malformed way of describing the situation. For though it is true that the Focus is bracketed, for example, in an account of the Eucharist, so likewise are the manifestations of the Focus as 'appearances'. Indeed it is not possible to disentangle the Focus from the way it is held to manifest itself and to operate within the manifest, in this case the sacramental bread and wine. If the Focus is bracketed so are the manifestations. It is thus artificial to draw a line between the 'appearances' studied by phenomenology and the reality which may or not lie behind them. It is true that I have made use of here the idea of a noumenal Focus, but this too is bracketed. So if one takes the bracketing with full seriousness, there is reason to reject the use of the term 'phenomena'. But as things are at present it remains a useful slogan, to indicate something about the presuppositions of phenomenological enquiry.

Now we can return to the problem of what could be meant by the interpolation of the 'phenomena' into our lives, of which van der Leeuw speaks.

The question has been much discussed, of course, in the context of the philosophy of history, by Dilthey, Collingwood, and others. However, it is worth noting that there is nothing in principle to differentiate the problem in the distances of space and time: that is, for the contemporary Englishman to understand the meaning of a twentieth century Vietnamese rite is a task not differing in principle from that involved in trying to understand the meaning of a twelfth-century English rite. It is true that with contemporaries there are vastly greater possibilities of obtaining information, and there is too the golden chance of talking with those participating in a rite. But in both cases, and irrespectively of space and time there is a *cultural* distance which has to be overcome. Thus it is quite as likely that we can learn methodologically from anthropology as it is that we can learn from history as a science.

The idea that the phenomenologist has to put himself in the other man's shoes, a rather crude characterisation of the Collingwoodian programme, runs up against an objection rather rudely expressed by Evans-Pritchard when castigating some of the better known theorists in the history of anthropology, that it commits the 'If-I-were-a-horse' fallacy [5]. Too often the theorist may try to imagine himself in a primitive environment (for example), coming up with absurd accounts of how primitives arrive at certain beliefs. What does the fallacy amount to?

It is, I think, this: that the theorist or observer operates as though he can travel on a kind of time-machine, that is, can arrive (imaginatively) in another culture and then go on thinking roughly according to the cultural modes of his own society. He takes his cultural baggage with him. But this is not, of course, what is required, for in order to understand what it is like to be, say, a Winnebago one must really make-believe that one is a Winnebago, rehearsing the thoughts and attitudes of a Winnebago, not of an Englishman planted in Winnebago territory.

Because of the organic nature of religious beliefs and practices – their interconnection in a fine web of relations – the process of sympathetic imagination involves something like learning a new language and it is therefore not just a matter of empathy. Or rather, empathy, if it is to be a fine-grained emotional and attitudinal identification with the participants of another faith, has to be structured in accord with the organic web.

I have spoken here as though the problem is essentially one of trans-cultural understanding. In one way it need not be, for our observers of the Anglican Eucharist might after all themselves be Anglicans. But typically the phenomenologist is involved in trans-cultural transactions for at least two reasons. First, his typological aims inevitably drive him to make judgements of comparison and contrast between different religions,

70

etc. Secondly, in evolving a moving picture of a faith, one is necessarily caught up with historical investigations; and there is a cultural gap, even within the tradition of one's own faith, between the contemporary picture and the pictures of past centuries. This indeed is why the phenomenon of milieu-transformation is of continued importance. It could also be added that even if a scholar were to devote himself exclusively to the study of a particular religion, say an English Buddhologist, it would be wise for him to make explicit comparisons between Buddhism and the Christianity of the Buddhologist's own culture. The reason for this is that nothing is more likely to produce distortions than to see another culture or religion in terms of one's own, and this is much more likely to happen where one's assumptions about religion are not brought to the surface and made explicit. The comparative exercise is the chief means of doing this. The principle no doubt extends further, for there are not only religious or anti-religious assumptions to take into account, but a whole milieu of presuppositions about what is rational and irrational, normal and abnormal, scientific and unscientific; and there can be a temptation, hard to resist, to project these contrasts upon another culture, one consequence of which is that other societies are depicted from a rationalist point-of-view. For instance, because so-called primitives use magic (incidentally a debatable concept, in its relation to religion), it has been held that they do not understand causality. So rationalist assumptions must be guarded against, in particular where they attempt to generate explanations of features of other cultures very different from those of our own society. This is not, incidentally, to say that Rationalism as a form of scientific humanism is wrong – it is indeed a possible even a respectable, *Weltanschauung*. But it is no more sound to suppose that primitives are irrational because they use magic than it is to think (on the basis of a Christian traditionalism) that Theravada Buddhism must be a depressing religion because it believes neither in a Creator nor in an immortal soul. In brief, then, it is important in the trans-cultural situation to bring assumptions as far as possible to the surface by the exercise of comparative judgements. This is a way to help liberate the phenomenologist form his own cultural background when he is

71

presenting to himself or others the religious facts which he is exploring.

A model of the phenomenologist's work is, perhaps, reading and assimilating a novel. Within the pages of the novel and in their own way, the brothers Karamazov exist, though in another way it does not matter whether they did or did not exist; typically it is not a question which needs asking. Prescinding, however, from the 'real' world, in a novel one is immersed in a particular ambience, and moves with the characters, play-acting their feelings, understanding their beliefs, beginning to live in their social world. It is not necessary to agree with Ivan Karamazov in 'real life': one still can see the world from his point-of-view, and likewise with Alyosha. They are two brothers with very different outlooks, One may not in real life actually sympathise with a given character, but within the world of the novel one can have a vivid empathy. (Perhaps, however, 'empathy' is too technical-sounding but 'sympathy' is too strong and does not signal the bracketing.)

The analogy with novel-reading is defective in one important way, nevertheless, for reading a novel is relatively unstrenuous work, especially if the author is a master of the art of absorbing the reader. On the other hand, phenomenological description is effortful 'hardy work' (to use a phrase of Eichhofen's), and in its own way creative, even if parasitic upon the creativity of religion itself in throwing up forms of belief, myth, rite. But the analogy has the merit of drawing attention to the fact that it is possible to enter into a certain social world, imaginatively, without accepting its presuppositions in reality and in a manner which can hold together mutually conflicting attitudes, each empathetically understood. It also has a certain realism as an analogy because so often, for contingent reasons, the phenomenologist is confronted by the written word – texts, descriptions, reports; but this situation is indeed only a typical occupational hazard. The anthropologist working in the field also indulges in his make-believe, entering into the community of his study so far as social and other conditions will allow, participating and observing at the same time, entering into human relations with the humans he is contemplating sociologically. Here the texts are transcended, just as the phenomenologist of contemporary

72

religion can enter into dialogue with its practitioners, not dependent on written and like sources such as stand in the way of the historian and the actual past. But since the phenomenologist, however much he may desire to participate in dialogue and ceremony, is typically comparative and trans-cultural in his operations, as also the anthropologist when he gets to theorising, he can only be fragmentarily in the condition of transcending the texts and reports.

Texts, incidentally, have loomed unnaturally large in the firmament of the history of religions. There are various reasons for this, if we are thinking in particular of sacred texts. First, sacred texts have been held to be normative (hence their sanctity, it could be said) for the traditions of some of the great religions, though the mode and degree of normativeness have varied considerably as between the religions. This it has been held that it is possible to reach the 'essence' of a faith by consideration of its scriptures (a somewhat misleading idea, as it does not account for the evolution of the community plus its practices as the living milieu of the texts in question). Second, it happens that the great burst of historical scholarship in the nineteenth century, which formed the matrix of the history of religions (Religion) itself, was heavily oriented towards philology; hence one could have the exuberant theory of the great Max Müller, that gods arose as an effect of a disease of language, *nomina numina*. Third, because of the *historical* impetus of the history of religions it has been natural to look backwards and work through the main traces of the past, namely written documents. Fourth, Religion has arisen chiefly, though by no means exclusively, in the circumstances of Protestant liberalism and its penumbra in the West, especially in northern Europe and also in the United States. This context both clearly and dimly incorporates the feeling that the Bible is the exclusive source of revelation and knowledge of the Focus, it thus being natural to think of other religions in an analogous manner. This in itself was no bad thing, for combined with philological concerns, it gave impetus to the great work of translating the 'sacred' documents of other faiths: consider, for instance, the great 'Sacred Books of the East', and consider also the magnificent editorial achievements of the Pali Text Society. Fifth, it

73

should be recognised that a major educational tradition in the West has been the classical one in which it has been a major enterprise to induct young people into the thought forms of the Graeco-Roman world through reading the great authors who wrote in Greek and Latin, especially in the preferred ages of the two cultures. It has not been unnatural to extend the same treatment to other cultures by trying to understand the Chinese through the Confucian and other classics, to approach India through the great Sanskrit works, and so on. It is only rather recently (and partly under American influence, since it was chiefly in the United States that the concept of area studies was evolved) that a rather different approach to other cultures has been undertaken. (Of course, anthropology never really followed the Great Tradition, mainly for want of written documents but also for other reasons. In turn, this was one factor in its unnatural division from sociology and from its isolation from classical and oriental studies in most educational institutions. This is sad of course, since it is only recently that more systematic attempts have been made to apply anthropological results to the study of classical and other myths). Finally, it is worth remarking that the study of theology itself has often been conceived on 'classical' (i.e., textual and philological) lines, especially in England, where this approach has been a means of compromise with the ethos of a largely secular university system, uncommitted to any Theology.

However, though there has been unnatural emphasis upon sacred texts, often in a situation where their real place in the life of the tradition has been imperfectly understood, it remains true that the phenomenologist has to work much of the time through documents. In unfavourable circumstances, this can create a vicious circle: inadequate phenomenology yielding unfortunate categories themselves used by those who report upon religions yielding inadequate phenomenology. But this is, of course, a merely contingent hazard of the trade.

I have endorsed the term 'empathy' for the affective side of the phenomenologist's 'entering into' the world of another religious culture, or even of his own. It is implicit in this use that it is not full-blown symathy in the ordinary way. It is true that a person works best at what he loves, and the lover of Buddhism will,

74

other things being equal, be a better scholar of Buddhism than one to whom it 'means nothing' as we say – that is, is cod-like in its lack of attraction. But if we are to take the bracketing operation seriously, it means that the phenomenologist *qua* phenomenologist is not endorsing Buddhism, expressing his sympathy for it, aligning himself with its values (though it is sometimes a useful pedagogical ploy in addressing an audience leaning too much the other way). For aligning oneself with Buddhism is a mild way of Expressing the *dharma*, and so in its modest manner is a form of Theologising (*Dharmologising*). Thus the presentation of Buddhism must itself remain emotionally bracketed, and thus does not amount to full sympathy as exhibited in 'real' life.

Such remarks may attract the criticism that I am crying for supermen, people who genuinely transcend their own culture in the enterprise of phenomenology. Surely there actually remains a high degree of social conditioning which can never be eliminated by the cry of 'bracketing'. We may in theory bracket questions of truth, but how can we in practice bracket matters of feeling and attitude? My answer to this is to go further along the line suggested by the analogy of the novel. I turn to playacting.

Certainly it will not be denied that good actors can present feelings and emotions, of love, hate, jealousy, ambition, disgust, chagrin, pride, meanness, courage, depression, elation, sadness, joy, apprehension, melancholy, nervousness, arrogance, humility, hypocrisy, carelessness, lackadaisicalness, ennui, nostalgia, and so forth. But it would be absurd to think that Oliver, who tonight portrays joy, ennui, lackadaisicalness, arrogance and sadness in 'The Cherry Orchard' is except contingently given these days to such emotions. (Or even if he is given to joy, it is joy directed at a different object or objects, such as joy that he has re-married or scored a great success or booked to go to Antibes next week.) The actor, therefore, succeeds in a quite practical manner in bracketing the emotions, dispositions, etc., which he presents on the stage. There can thus be no *a priori* reason why the phenomenologist should not imaginatively rehearse the feelings and beliefs of those he aims evocatively to describe and should not go on to set his results down on paper,

75

or through some other mode of expression (for it is by no means a dogma or even pedagogically sound to suppose that the chief instrument of phenomenology must always be the written word).

Thus the phenomenologist, in so far as he is presenting a structural description of a faith at a certain time or an item therein organically related to its contextual items is typically making use of empathetic imagination, and this involves a bracketing of feelings and attitudes in the phenomenologist himself. This presumably is what is meant by 'interpolating a phenomenon into one's life'. Of course also substantially, and in an unbracketed way, there may result a change in the phenomenologist's attitudes; he may, for instance, come to be critical of Theologians in his own cultural tradition who do not take other religions seriously; or he may come to be attracted by certain values in other religions, such as Ghandi's interpretations of non-violence or the Buddhist attitude to right speech. This would be, so to say, an educational effect of his occupation. But these *substantial* changes in attitude, vital as they might be in creating a new humanism which does not rest solely on the values of the Western tradition and which counteracts the despisal of other cultures so prominent in the colonial and post-colonial phases of European history, are not the primary aim of phenomenology as a method.

Trickier and more debatable is the second phase of phenomenology, when one moves from the structural description and presentation of a particular item, such as the Anglican Eucharist, in the organic context of a particular tradition, to the work of typology. The emphasis that I have already placed on the organic interconnections of items in a religion surely makes it virtually impossible to make worth-while comparisons. If so, the project especially of a general phenomenology, such as that undertaken by Gerardus van der Leeuw is illusory. Before treating this topic let us recapitulate briefly the points or point of making comparisons and contracts.

First, if there are similarities in apparently independent cultures it is suggestive that we might arrive at an explanation of these convergences. This *could* be broadly an historical explanation. At one time, for instance, it was thought that the *Bhaga-*

vad-Gita must have been influenced by Christianity. Dumézil's work on gods and society in Indo-European societies has an historical dimension also [6]. The explanation *could* be structural, and either internal or external (in the sense indicated in last chapter). Thus the similarities of Śankara's and Eckhart's doctrines (though not *tremendously* close, but sufficiently so) could be accounted for structurally in terms of types of religious experience and sentiment. This would be an internal explanation. The similarities between mother-goddesses in different cultures might be accounted for by the prevalence of similar types of agricultural arrangements.

If similarities are suggestive, so of course are dissimilarities. It is a matter of importance, for instance, that Theravada Buddhism does not involve a supreme personal Being, when this belief not only became prevalent in Hinduism but also is widely found in the major religious traditions.

To some extent a typology will be guided by the interests of possible kinds of explanation, but leaving this aside and concentrating on what constitutes the 'pure' task of phenomenological classification, we can first note that one kind of categorisation is according to kinds of activities, notably rites. Thus prayers, sacrifices, sacraments, initiations, hymnsinging, pilgrimages, funerals, fasts, yogic practices, celebrations of feastdays, and so forth are (sometimes overlapping) practices discoverable in the ritual dimension of religion. As will be seen shortly not all the categories are free from criticism and debate, but it is not unreasonable, despite the organic character of each religious tradition, to apply these categories within different cultures. One major reason for this possibility is that in an important sense these categories are formal rather than material, if a new use of the scholastic distinction may be permitted. By this I mean that in saying that someone is praying one is not so far indicating the fine grain of his activity, which substantially derives from his conception of the Focus of his prayers. Prayer is the form of his activity: the matter is the intention as directed towards a particular Focus. Somewhat similarly, if one says that a person is complaining, one is describing the form of his activity, but so far have not made reference to what he is complaining *about*.

77

Such formal categories can work within limits, even if there are recurring problems of particularity. Thus 'the Eucharist' is a phrase we would be chary of using outside the Christian tradition to categorise a sacred meal, because the term carries with it close implication with the material element (even more obviously does 'the Lord's Supper'); but 'sacrament' is more ambivalent. Though defined in a certain way, or ways, in Christian theology and confined to a limited number of sacred activities, there is between, say, marriage in the Christian tradition as a sacrament and marriage in the Hindu tradition, also given sacred and symbolic significance. Here and elsewhere it is necessary to recognise that to some extent phenomenological categories become abstractions from the formal aspects of varying practices; or, as it is sometimes put, 'ideal types'.

The formal–material distinction can be worked within limits also in relation to experiences and sentiments (for example, the sense of the numinous, the sense of spiritual peace, etc., can be indicated without referring to the particular) and with regard to institutional roles (priest, layman, shaman, prophet, etc.). And at another level, my categorisation of different dimensions of religion (doctrinal, mythic, etc.) is a formal one. Since the anatomy of the Focus (or Foci) of a religion or religious activity is delineated, so to say, primarily in the mythic and doctrinal aspects of a tradition, it will be useful to explore the mythic in more detail, and to this I now turn.

3 The Mythic Firmament

Common as it may be to define religion by reference to belief in God, gods, etc. (a procedure which runs up against troubles in any case in regard to, for example, Theravada Buddhism), there may be merit in looking at the Focus or Foci of religious activity through the medium of the mythic, that is, in a context where such entities are *acting*, not just so to say quietly existing. It is also useful to achieve as much clarity as is at present possible on the nature of the mythic in view of the many debates about the functions, existential, social, and so forth of myths. To some extent my procedure will be prescriptive, that is, defining myth in a manner suiting my argument.

The first thing that needs repeating is, of course, that to categorise something as a myth is *not* to assert that it is false. It is unfortunate that in the English language (and others) the word has attracted the meaning of 'false story' or more broadly 'false account'. We have in part to thank the Greeks for this development, in part too the Church – for early apologists could contrast the true story of God's saving work in Israel and in Christ with the 'myths' of the pagans. It is of course easy to think that one's own myth is a true story, the other man's myth is a myth. It is, then, vitally important to rid our minds of any suggestion that the mythic is *qua* mythic false or merely fanciful. It may turn out that all myths are false, but on the usage adopted here this is contingent, for the usage leaves open the possibility of speaking of true myths.

Crudely, the distinction I wish to draw between a myth and a doctrine is that the latter has to do with the constitution of the world, of the transcendent, etc., while the former has to do with a moving picture of the sacred. This crude distinction will no doubt have to be heavily qualifid in due course, but I wish to bring out the first major characteristic of myth,

79

namely that it is a form of *story*. It belongs in a genus which includes also novels, jokes, fairy-stories, historical narratives, though as will be seen there can be overlaps between the species (for instance, some myths are historical narratives).

But how does one, broadly, differentiate myths from other kinds of stories? Is it, for instance, in terms of their *material* reference, to God or gods, for example? This will not quite do, for the story of the Buddha's conquest of Mara in the Pali canon concerns two persons, the Buddha and Mara, neither of whom are strictly gods. To define myths materially, it would be necessary to expand the list of beings with which they typically deal: God, gods, evil spirits, culture heroes, primeval men, sacred eggs. But maybe the list could be simplified by taking into account two points.

First, sacred and numinous beings typically split into two forms, good and evil, holy and 'unholy' (I do not use the term to refer to the profane or the non-holy, but the threatening type of *mysterium tremendum*, to use Otto's terminology). I shall return in a moment to elaborate this point. Meanwhile, second, myths typically have to do with the relationship between the transcendent, the supernatural, etc. (but these terms are inadequate) on the one hand and man and the world on the other. Thus although a culture hero or a primeval man may appear in a myth, he does so in a way related to the sacred.

Unfortunately, there are troubles of a terminological kind in trying to find a generic term to cover the holy and the 'unholy' beings referred to just now. Indeed the situation is fairly complicated in terms of the good–evil split. For with regard to a being of this kind, either he is the object of worship or, oppositely, he is dreaded but renounced, as with the Devil in the Christian tradition. (Also some gods can become otiose, no longer figuring significantly in the cultus, but let us leave this point on one side.) But it is not necessarily the case that the sacred splits into accepted and renounced beings, since it is also possible for the good–evil dichotomy to be preserved within the substance of a being who is worshipped, as with Kali. Further a god may have, so to say, offshoots, not directly objects of worship but partaking in some of the holy power of their originator, like angels in the Christian tradition; likewise

80

there can be lesser demons performing the work of an Evil one. It is hard to know what generic term should be used both for beings that are worshipped and those that are numinous, but renounced – gods and antigods [1]. Somewhat artificially I shall use the term 'divinities' to mean both and to cover their minor offshoots [2]. On this usage the Christian tradition has involved belief in a number of divinities, including good and evil angels, but only one God (for only one divinity is worshipped, and he is supreme).

We may then define myths *materially* as stories concerning divinities, typically in relationship to men and the world. It will later be necessary to say something about the style of myths, for this in part derives from conceptions about the spaces and times which divinities inhabit. However, first it is important to enquire about the point of telling such stories. Of course, we all like a good story, and it is notable that the *Mahabharata* and the *Ramayana*, which are mythic epics, have become a basic source of entertainment for the Indian masses. But it cannot be said that the prime function of the telling of a myth is entertainment. It is indeed already a sign that a story is being transmuted out of the mythic mode when it is worked up into epic form or repeated as folklore or fairy-tales. The primary context of the telling of a myth is ritual, in which the reality of the events and transactions between divinities and men is re-enacted, or in some cases *pre*-enacted, for myths can concern the future as well as the past. Myths thus typically are celebrations, though not all celebrations incorporate myths. The celebration of the Incarnation occurs at Christmas, for instance, when Christ is, so to say, born again in our midst.

The celebratory, ritual milieu of myth-telling means that there are analogues to myth in primarily 'secular' contexts, that is, where the material of the myth is not divinities. For instance, the celebration of the October Revolution makes real again the founding event and the guarantee of the triumph of Communism.

Thus we have so far distinguished myths as being concerned with divinities and as typically occurring in a celebratory, ritual context. Both marks of a myth have to be taken 'seriously'. For instance, though children celebrate Christmas in a certain sense by waiting for and receiving the gifts of Father Christmas, who might seem *prima facie* to qualify as a divinity, in fact (in England at any rate) Father Christmas has lapsed largely into a fairy-story. It does not matter too much if he is seen to be a mere fiction. But the genuine myth takes its divinities much more seriously and concretely.

One also needs to distinguish a myth from a *parable*, even though the latter may typically concern divinities. A major mark of the parable is that it is normally a literal tale about ordinary incidents, such as searching for lost money or helping the victim of robbery or having people to a big dinner or trying to get children out of a burning house [3]. It is about divinities, but obliquely: the divinities do not occur as such in the matter of the parable. The parable tends to be illustrative, rather than material for re-enactment in a celebratory context. It is true that sometimes myths can come to be treated more-or-less as parables, as happens often today with the story of Adam and Eve, which is now treated not as a myth of 'actual' events, but as a story illustrating the existential relationship between God and men. It becomes thus something ex-mythic, more parable-like.

A feature of many myths is their 'explanatory' power. I put the word in quotation marks to distinguish the style of explanation from that available in modern science and history (for example). The so-called aetiological myths give an account of, and a kind of legitimation of, ritual and social practices, while cosmogonic myths 'explain' the world in a manner which relates it to the transactions between men and divinities. The attempt to back such explanations scientifically – to find in modern astronomy, through the 'Big Bang' cosmology, for instance, a vindication of the Genesis creation myth – both affirms and betrays the spirit of the mythic 'explanation'. It affirms it in seeking a concrete aspect of the 'truth' of the myth and in connecting our investigations with the divinity portrayed in the myth; but it betrays it in trying to transpose it into another key. In this respect metaphysical explanation, such as that exhibited in natural theology, is nearer to the spirit of mythic explanation. For the natural sciences have nothing to do with celebrations and ritual, while natural

82

theology at least wrestles with the question of whether after all it has to do with the God of Abraham, the living God [4].

The connection between myth and ritual is not surprising in view of the manner in which the gods are characterised, for they are the divinities attracting worship (while their antibodies, the devils, attract a kind of anti-worship, a renunciation and warding-off of their influence, mythically reflected in the struggle between good and evil in heaven and upon earth, etc.). Thus the matter of myths has to do with Foci of ritual, or in other words, worship and its attendants, such as sacrifice. It should not therefore seem odd that myth and ritual go together, typically.

The characterisation of myth so far given does not preclude it from referring to historical events. For transactions between divinities and men can occur quite historically, and how indeed should they occur in any other way? But a *caveat* is necessary. For we in the twentieth century have arrived at a certain understanding of the historical method and so have reasonably well-defined views as to what could and could not have actually happened. Moreover, we use the phrase 'historical events' to refer to events that did indeed happen in history. But if we are to pursue the method of phenomenological bracketing, we must not, in understanding the historical aspect of some myths, let these twentieth-century assumptions get in the way of understanding. First, from a phenomenological point of view there is no difference in kind between an event that did happen and an event that did not happen but is believed or 'known' to have happened. Both belong, phenomenologically, in the same category, both are treated as historical. Second, the fact that we might rule something out now as being historically impossible (say, Lazarus' rising from the dead) does not show that such an event was not treated in a relevant sense as historical in an earlier epoch. The event can be pictured, it is believed unquestioningly, it belongs to the flow of human events, which forms the fabric of history. Thus it is wrong to convert a judgement of truth into a judgement of phenomenological category. For this reason it is not possible to define myth negatively by reference to historicity or to what is scientifically possible. However, we *then* have the problem of differentiating any myths which are *not* 'historical', since on the present account they chiefly concern transactions between divinities and men. True, cosmogonic myths and myths of the genealogies and battles of the divinities may be once-removed from human affairs; but what of myths of the first ancestors and the like? Should not these be treated in the same category as 'hard' historical myths, such as the story of God's leading Israel out of Egypt?

Some attempt is made by Mircea Eliade to get over this problem by distinguishing between sacred and profane time, between *illud tempus*, the Grand Time, in which mythic events occurred, and profane time, the time experienced chronologically [5]. He also distinguishes between the cyclical and linear notions of time, the former characteristic of myth and ritual, repeating the Eternal Present, the latter characteristic of the Judaeo-Christian tradition. In part, it seems to me, Eliade is right: there is a way in which some myths express an indefinite past time, *illud tempus*, especially those dealing with cosmogony and the beginnings of the human predicament, etc. And equally we speak of an indefinite future, the eschatological consummation or restoration of things. Thus both *Urzeit* and *Endzeit* are temporally rather indefinite, so much so that when the attempt is made to fix a date, say, for Armageddon, there are many dates to choose from, and they can be revised. But one needs a firm criterion of what counts as a *linear* view of time.

If it is ritual repetition which makes for a cyclical notion, then certainly the Christian tradition entertains the latter, for the Lord's Supper is re-enacted with great frequency. If it is a belief in cycles of history that makes for the cyclical view, then many ethnic religions do not have it, for they do not indulge in the cosmology of *kalpas*, rebirths, etc., such as characterises the Indian tradition and parts of the ancient Greek. If it is a sense of particular dating (or equivalent devices) in retelling the story of the faith which makes for a linear view, then Buddhism has this, not only in the story of the Buddha's life but also in such chronicles as the *Mahavamsa* and the *Culavamsa* (while even the fabulous *Jatakas* go in for a sort of dating: 'When X was king of Y', and so forth). Further, eschatological

84

notions, though they may not be prominent in Indian religions, certainly exist there, and there has been scarcely a more historically conscious culture outside the West than China. It must then be concluded that the distinction which Eliade wishes to present cannot properly be substantiated. But we can do something with the suggestion that the 'times' of certain myths are characteristically indefinite, notably those of the *Urzeit* and the *Endzeit*. To this extent it is possible to make a distinction between myths which treat their time 'historically' and those which do not (but even here the distinction needs to be qualified: consider the way the Creation myth in Genesis merges into the chronological generations which lead into the chronicle of the nation of Israel).

If there are problems about time, there are also problems about space. If myths are not always chronological, but take place in a strange time at the beginning or at the end of time, they also involve a dislocation, sometimes, of space. Or let us say that space is not always quite literally presented, but has its discontinuities. This has to do with the location of the divinities (using this term in my technical sense) and with the tendencies of mythic cosmology. This latter phrase is perhaps not entirely appropriate, since I have defined the mythic partly through the idea of a story, the moving picture of divinities; yet the mythic world itself has as certain background elements a cosmology – not in the strict sense a scientific one (even if occasionally protoscientific cosmologies arise or coalesce from mythic ones in strange ways). Thus I would prefer a somewhat different term. As it so happens that there are well-known correspondences in the mythic and religious milieux between the macrocosm and the microcosm, and since an important aspect of the latter is the human being, and since there are also well-developed 'mythic' physiologies and psychologies in different cultures (such as the Kundalini idea in the Yoga tradition), it is convenient to use the terms 'macrocosmology' and microcosmology' to refer to these two different aspects of the delineation of reality as a background to mythic events. One also needs to speak of a kind of geography as a mean between these two aspects; for instance, the 'mythic' geography of Jambudvipa and the centrality of Mount Meru in

85

the classical Indian tradition. The sacred geography, for the sake of a term, may conveniently be referred to as ' mesocosmology'. So, then, we may ask what are the locations of mythic events?

As already indicated they can occur importantly upon this earth, in the mesocosmological sphere; thus Adam and Eve occupied the Garden of Eden, which is indefinitely locatable. But some occur more concretely within known places, lying at or near the centre of a mesocosm, such as the birth of Christ in Bethlehem, the exploits of Krishna at Brindaban, the actions of the gods upon Olympus. One might make a roughly similar distinction to that which I canvassed earlier in relation to time: while some mythic events occur in indefinite time, notably at the beginning and the end of our epoch or of human history as a whole, so some mythic events can occur definitely in a certain known place within the mesocosm, while others occur more indefinitely on its fringes. But space has more than one dimension, while time, so to say, does not. There could at most be three times – definite, indefinite, and the eternal (and the last is a kind of no-time); but space extends beyond the definite, the indefinite, and the transcendent no-space. Or rather, between the mesocosm and no-space (the transcendent) there can lie (in the upward direction) heaven or a series of layers of heavenly spheres, while below the earthly mesocosm there can be a succession of purgatories and hells. Sometimes these other places can merge into those identified in lateral directions, such as the Pure Land to the West, famous in the Mahayana Buddhist scriptures, which has the attributes of a heaven, though figured mesocosmically but so far out of the mesocosm as to become part of the macroscosm. Thus the indefinite parts of the mesocosm merge into the macrocosm, while the definite parts bring us nearer home.

It is, in these terms, possible to define those myths which have an historical content (using this 'still' in the bracketed sense, thus prescinding from questions of historical accuracy and the like) as referring to transactions between divinities and men in the definite part of the mesocosm and a definite segment of time. To put it crudely, they latch on to dates and places, even if these dates and places may be hard to determine by modern methods of historical research. Thus Indra led the

Aryans into battle to destroy the forts of the dark-skinned Dasyus, but was this the set of campaigns which destroyed the Indus Valley civilisation? It perhaps is not even important to determine the historical accuracy of such myths, for they still retain their status as phenomenological objects despite conclusions about truth. We here attempt to describe their style.

But many myths tell of occurrences which take place in and beyond the macrocosm when, for instance, the gods battle amongst themselves, or when Satan becomes a fallen angel. Still, in view of the existential nisus of the mythic, portraying the interaction between divinities and men, many myths take place in the region of the mesocosm, with ascent and descent from and to it.

The fact that in re-enacting the myth, or in taking part in rituals to which a given myth is relevant, one time is represented in another (the first Easter, for instance, being re-created here and now in the Easter celebrations; and men sing 'Jesus Christ is risen *today*') is echoed by the possibility of one place being present in another, as when all rivers are somehow the Ganges. But mythic space is essentially more complex than mythic time, because macrocosmology is linked to the differentiation of divinities: heavens, for instance, being spaces occupied by gods, and regions below the mesocosm being the typical habitations of demonic powers. Thus another world (in and beyond the macrocosm) can be present in this world, as *brahman*, for instance, the power sustaining and informing the whole macrocosm is also especially present in the Vedic sacrifices, or as in the descent of divinities to the earthly plane, trailing clouds of their upper glory.

The fact that myths are re-told indicates that what they describe is somehow repeatedly available; to understand one aspect at least of this it is useful to look at the dynamics of the divinities. I propose here to sketch a crude model which may illuminate mythic identities, polarities, etc.

A divinity has certain properties or powers, either intrinsic or acquired through mythic action. I shall use the term 'powers', since there is a tendency for properties to be treated almost as detached entities. Consider for instance the semi-autonomous status of the *Amesha Spentas* in Zoroastrianism, or the way in which God's activities can be figured as angels, or the way in which the *śakti* or creative power of God in the Indian tradition detaches itself as the female counterpart to the male divinity. The term 'powers' is more suggestive of this detachability. It also contains the suggestion of parts or elements rather than of adjectival properties, a point which will prove of some importance in the succeeding analysis.

Much ink has been spilled in trying to characterise so-called 'primitive thinking', which in large part amounts to the attempt to spell out the logic of mythic and ritual thinking. There are obvious ways in which the account I shall give owes much to these discussions, but I do not wish directly to enter into dialogue here with Lévi-Strauss or Lévy-Bruhl or others. It is hoped, however, that the principles I outline, though simplified, go some way to making sense of myth and ritual.

The first principle to be enunciated (which covers more than the actions and effects of divinities) is that manifestations of similar powers are manifestations of an identical power. That is, different entities and occurrences manifesting a given characteristic, such as fieriness, manifest a single power, such as Fire. Every fire participates in Fire. We may call this the principle of power-identity.

Clearly much depends upon the criteria for classifying things together as having the same power. For if X is like Y then it will be thought to manifest the same power. But what are the relevant respects in which X is like Y? Here there is wide room for maneouvre, which becomes important when we come to deal with 'symbolic' actions and entities. Let us enunciate, however, a second principle, that where two entities or occurrences are relevantly alike in respect of some sign, they possess the same power (as signified by the sign). The world is, so to say, such that a power spreads to occupy anything of a given kind. We may call this the principle of likeness.

Of course it is necessary to bear in mind that often the signs of likeness are contradictory and here the entities in question are liable to be especially dangerous. Also it is to be expected that a power may exist with greater intensity in one entity or set of entities than in others. To this point we shall return.

88

Powers may be crudely characterised as being good, bad, and neutral (but I'll leave the neutral case aside in the following account for the sake of simplicity), primarily in relation to human beings, but not exclusively by any means. For one needs to see the mythic–ritual *Weltanschauung* as being seamless, a network of relationships which apply equally to both human and non-human events. A good power, looking at the matter anthropocentrically, brings advantage to some group of humans, through some transaction occurring in given conditions. Thus fire transmits heat to food which is being cooked. In other conditions, however, the same power may be dangerous, for fire can burn down a hut or in the form of lightning can kill. It is therefore necessary to discriminate not only the sign of the power, but also the sign of the benefit-bringing conditions.

It is an assumption contained in the notion that there are good and bad powers that in some sense these powers transmit themselves in certain conditions or through certain points of contact. In virtue of the principle of likeness there is thus a resemblance of the effect and the cause. The power of fire transmits heat to colder bodies, which thus acquire the power of the transmitter. Where such an acquisition of transmitted power is dangerous, the object is to avoid the appropriate contact or to generate in the situation a means of blocking the transmission. This is, so to say, a way of keeping a situation stable.

Before applying some of the above remarks more concretely to ritual and myth, one further observation needs to be made, namely that a given power may be held more intensely by one entity rather than by another (the sun, for instance possesses fire more intensely than my hearth). But some mechanism, whether natural or cultural, needs to exist to maintain such superior intensity, otherwise the power becomes dissipated equally among like entities. However, the causal or creative relation between X and Y implies the superior power of X; and anything which maintains itself as generative of a power in others displays the superior intensity of its power.

I shall now apply some of these principles to some simple ritual contexts. Consider a person approaching his chief:

person P salutes C (the chief), who may acknowledge the salute. What is the meaning of the salutation? It is not simply a matter of gratifying the chief's vanity (though it may do that). The salutation occurs because the chief is chief, not because he is vain. We may represent the explanation as being something like this: the occasion is of contact between P and C, where C possesses the power of action or causing action within the group more intensely than P. But both P and C share group membership; by the principle of likeness C's power would tend to spread to P, and an equalisation to occur. The salute however is a sign of unlikeness, of the distinction between C and P. Another sign is the acknowledgment; or the distinctive badges of C; or the fact that C sits in a more elevated position. To notice such badges is to give the salute, so that the various signs are intrinsically connected. The salute itself maintains the *status quo* – the act of approach might put the badges in jeopardy, but the salute maintains them.

What it is important to notice about this simple act of ritual is that the salute as a sign of unlikeness and of the superior power of the chief is itself *part* of that superior power. Consider what happens if P fails to produce the sign. If such indifference or insolence is left unpunished the authority of C is to that extent diminished. The damage to his power has to be compensated by a further act, one of humiliating P, as well as indicating the pain and damage liable to be suffered by anyone else failing to produce the sign. In brief, a ritual sign can be part of the power of which it is a sign.

This means that it is wrong to treat signs merely as 'symbolising' something. Driven snow is said to symbolise purity, and it might be all right, if trite, to paint a picture of a maiden enveloped in driven snow to symbolise a certain kind of purity. However, the driven snow is not part of her purity, but in an important sense the badges of the chief, his fly-whisk, say, are part of his being chief. He is invested with them, and they can of course be taken away by a counter-ritual.

The principle of likeness helps us to understand why it is that signs appear to be symbolic: for the sign as being part of the power of which it is a sign, and being often a cultural object, is in some respect like that which it signifies, or at least

90

this is frequently and naturally so. It has an analogy to the sign signified of which it is also, by likeness and in practice, a part. Thus the height of a king's throne is a sign of the way in which the king in virtue of his function is set 'over' his people. However, as was said earlier, there is very considerable room for manoeuvre in the selection of signs, since their choice is determined by significant resemblance or analogy, and the respects in which resemblance might be seen are many.

The case of the chief is 'secular', in the sense that no special religious or sacred value need be attached to chiefdom. Let us turn now more particularly to sacred rituals. The celebration of Easter may do as an example. About this, several things are obvious but they need to be understood in their mutual relationship. First, there was only one Easter day – that is the Resurrection was a unique event. Second, from the point-of-view of those participating in the Easter celebrations, Christ truly rose from the dead (we need not worry here about the historicity of the Resurrection). We are concerned here with the phenomenology of it from the point-of-view of the faithful. Third, there is an important way in which the Resurrection is re-presented to the faithful, say on Easter Day, 1970. Fourth the celebration of Easter involves a ritual. Fifth, during, or as part of, the ritual, the story of Easter is retold.

Now it is certainly not enough to say that the telling of the Easter story is intended as an *explanation* of the continuance of the celebration. It is not enough to say this because the Easter story is in a way the *object* of the celebration, its content, as it were. Thus if someone declares 'We rejoice today because Jesus Christ rose from the dead' (or more significantly 'is risen from the dead'), he is expressing rejoicing *at* the Resurrection. This is rather different from 'We exchange eggs at Easter because originally eggs were a symbol of fertility, relevant at the major Spring festival.' Thus the telling of the Easter story is an enactment serving as the focus of the celebration.

But even so, the enactment still does more than a drama might. After all, in the theatre the main object of repeating what occurred tonight on the next and subsequent nights as well is to recreate the object to be contemplated so that it is available to further audiences. If the audience is big enough, as on television, it may not be important to repeat the drama. But the enactment of the Easter story in telling and in ritual makes the original event present once again. Note that it is the *event* which is re-presented, namely the Resurrection and Christ's triumph over death (on our behalf). Thus the myth and ritual enacted at Easter is held to correspond to the original event, to be a kind of replica of it. It is of course a replica with a difference, or better we might say that it is an analogical replica perhaps most dramatically expressed in the Eastern Orthodox liturgy. Why is its being a replica important? Because by the principles of likeness and power-identity, the power of the original event is identified with the power of the enactment.

The Easter celebration meets certain conditions of crucial resemblance: it occurs at the same time of year (or what is calculated to be); there is a correspondence between the telling and the event; and it participates, as do other communions, in the living power of Christ as saviour. In this last item, of course, a further analysis in terms of analogical likeness and power-identity has to be given. Thus Christ in blessing the bread and wine and uttering certain words over them authoritatively invested their resemblances to flesh and blood with his real presence. Thus they were 'possessed' by him, so that his power and theirs fused in such a manner that it was transmitted by eating to the disciples, and by repetition to the ever-widening circle of the faithful.

The myth and ritual of Easter, then, are replicas of what is taken to be the original event. It needs, though, to be stressed that the original event retains superior significance: it is a condition of the rest. For at least two reasons it is the fount from which the replicas flow. First, it is, as has been said, part of the content of the enactment (the latter has both a past and a present tense and could not exist on the latter alone). Second, the Resurrection is a demonstration of the divinity of Christ, from which the authority of the cultus flows. Thus it demonstrates the locus of the creative or generative power making the cultus possible. And as we have remarked earlier, the creative relation between X and Y implies the superior power of the creator (X) [7].

92

Given the principle of power-identity there is nothing especially mysterious or illogical in the notion that the risen Christ is present at Easter after Easter. For it is a feature of natural forces that they manifest themselves at different times. Thus fire can be re-kindled at different times, and cows yield milk this year as they did last. Divine forces can operate in the same manner.

What is true of time can also be said of space. Thus the Resurrection occurred in Palestine, but is re-presented in Rome, Athens, and London. There is still, however, a superior power in the original place, and this is a main motive for pilgrimage.

The authority of the original event helps to explain why it is that so many myths look back to primordial or founding events. But there is no reason in principle why the same 'real presence' should not flow from the future as well as from the past. Indeed this is the function of eschatological myths. The final overcoming of evil by God for example is, a future event in which we can participate now. If faith is the attitude which acknowledges our assured participation in the past, hope is the attitude acknowledging our assured participation in the future.

The relationship between a myth and a ritual which we have here been seeking to establish amounts to this: that the myth, uttered as an element in the ritual, is the central aspect of the way in which the original event is replicated. By the principle of likeness, the words theselves as uttered contain something of the power of the original. This feature of sacred language is characteristically applied to names of sacred and numinous objects, which thus become signs or parts of what they stand for.

This point can be used to illustrate an important aspect of mythic–ritual action. As we have seen, the ritual must be relevantly like the original (for example, occurring at the same time of the year). That is to say, elements in it, such as the utterance of the myth, must occur under the correct conditions. Similarly, invoking the name of God must occur in the correct conditions. Where it does not, for example, where it occurs in a context of levity and disrespect, the utterance becomes blasphemous. There is something dangerous about blasphemy

93

and if this can be explicated it may throw further light on the dynamics of the divinities who figure in myths.

In so far as a divinity displays numinous properties, and exhibits the *mysterium tremendum et fascinans* of which Rudolf Otto speaks, there exists a polarity between it and the worshipper. Although men can be deemed in some traditions to become superior to gods in power (consider how the exercise of austerity, *tapas*, can make the yogi more powerful than the gods; or how the Buddha is 'god above gods' though not a god [8]), we can begin with the more typical case of the god who is regarded as superior. The supreme case of this, of course, is, since all creative power is ultimately concentrated in him, the one God of monotheistic faiths. In so far as a god is superior the model of the salutation of the chief applies, though as we shall see a further element has to be introduced into the account which differentiates the god case from the chief case. But let us begin by applying the salutation model.

Whenever there is occasion for a person to address the god, a kind of contact is established. It is like the approach of the person to where the chief is seated. Often this has, of course, an almost literal side to it, where the god is specially present in an image in a sacred building. But even where there is less sense of this 'physical' location of the god, the model of approach applies, in so far as a person addresses the god. Given the superior power of the god, the same mechanism has to come into operation as applied in the chief case – a salutation (such as praise) is a sign of the difference between the person and the god. It is a sign indeed of the god's power, part of which is the capacity to exact praise. To this the numinous experience is, incidentally, relevant, for the awe-inspiring nature of the object of that experience proceeds 'naturally' to exact expression of awe. The use of language reverentially in the salutation is correct; the incorrect use, showing disrespect or unconcern, typifies blasphemy. This in principle is dangerous, for the maintenance of the god's status and power after this damage calls for the punishment and humiliation of the offender. Whatever may happen on the supernatural or natural planes, the group will tend to take strong action. By the principle of likeness the group and the blasphemer belonging to it are in a

94

sense united in power, and so the power of the blasphemous act itself might be thought to leak over into the community. The blasphemer can be ritually excluded from the group, for instance, with all the disadvantages this would imply. Such exclusion is ritualised because a sign of the unlikeness of the offender to the group has to be established over and against the present situation of his likeness and membership of the group.

Incidentally, one may go on to explain in this fashion the conditions in which the offender may be readmitted to the group. The ordinary mode of saluting the god might be considered the normal degree of reverence required in approaching the god. The degree to which the blasphemy falls below this determines the degree it must be exceeded in any penitential act.

The type of supernatural or natural danger which blasphemy might attract, apart from the action of the worshipping group against the offender, must of course in some degree depend upon the nature of the god addressed. A god whose power is associated with and manifests itself in crops may fail to generate the crops. Gods are not conceived at random, even if there is wide room for manoeuvre in the selection of features of the human environment to be endowed with divine and sacred significance (thus a god of maize can exist in central America but not in Asia, where maize does not grow). One cannot to this degree enunciate laws as to the necessary characteristics of the gods: even where patterns recur, they tend to do so in a contingent way. For example, sun gods and moon gods are widely attested, for the sun and moon shine on all men, but that there is but one moon and one sun is, so to say, a geographical accident of our earthly environment. Still, though the powers of the gods are numerously diverse and often highly particularised, in accord with the situation of their worshippers, it is possible to generalise about their essentially numinous character. Though not all Foci of religious aspiration are numinous, it is quite appropriate to categorise the divine Foci thus. The numinous power of a god induces sacred fear, and this is ambivalent towards human beings (and in principle other entities). The ambivalence can help to explain both the

95

dynamics of divine-human encounters and the nature of evil and maleficent forces existing in the spectrum of divinities (in the sense explained earlier).

The numinous induces sacred fear, or awe. Let us assume for the purpose of argument that the fear-inspiring power which it evinces is in principle beneficial, for example that it manifests eternal life, which can overcome death. This salvific potentiality, coupled with the awesomeness of the power, sets up a dialectic. On the one hand, the worshipper appropriately recognises his difference from the god: while the latter is holy and eternal, he is unholy or sinful and short-lived, subject to death. On the other hand, the recognition of the beneficial properties of the god impels the worshipper to hope to share something of the god's salvific power. For the power to spread to him, by the principle of likeness, he must somehow conform to the god's nature, at a lower and analogical level no doubt. By purifying himself and putting away his sin, he can achieve that conformity (or in some theologies it is ultimately achieved for him, by the grace of the god). Thus he exists simultaneously as recognising his unlikeness to the god and as aspiring to a kind of likeness. Assuming that the numinous power of the god is intense, the inferiority of the worshipper, even when he conforms himself by significant actions and sentiments to the likeness of the god, will imply his essential difference ontologically from the god; this, to put it simply, is the main root of all dualistic theologies, where god and man are seen as distinct. Indeed, the ontological difference means that the holiness acquired by man will be ascribed to the sole efficacy of the god, by his grace. Nevertheless, in this dialectic of likeness and unlikeness the worshipper does share in some sense in the holy power of the god.

There are many changes to be rung on this theme. The difference between the god and men, and the dangerousness of approaching the god profanely, may lead to the creation of a specialised class of person, priests, who are themselves set apart from the rest of people by virtue of special training, purification, austerity, or capacity for significant kinds of ecstatic experience, and whose function is to deal directly with the god or gods, mediating between them and the people. Again the

96

place of the god may be set apart, to limit approaches, in such a way that certain conditions of purity and sacredness have to be met by those stepping on the holy terrain round the god or entering the holy of holies. Similarly the times of approach may be limited, and conditions set, again, for purification, as in the prayer life of the Muslim.

It is the essence of the above dialectic that some benefit flowing form the numinous power depends on two conditions: the recognition of the power of and the conformity of the supplicant to at least an analogue of the holiness of the god. I have left the word 'recognition' here intentionally ambiguous. For one can recognise, that is to say note, something as dangerous or powerful without acknowledging it (by saluting and admiring it). It is the second that is the substance of recognising the power in the relevant ritual sense. However, I would prefer to use 'ritual recognition' somewhat more generally, as we shall shortly see, to include also the ritual relevant to a power considered maleficent. For I hope to show that both pro- and anti-rituals follow the same logic.

The fact that the blessing of the god accrues upon certain conditions (whether created by him or by men is irrelevant) points to the other side of the coin, when the conditions are not met. Now in principle the failure to meet the conditions might have a neutral result; but it is more characteristic for the failure to result in the opposite of blessing, some kind of disaster. The reasons for this are several. First, the sacred and profane represent a disjunction, and so with pure and impure, holy and unholy. It is true that, for instance, in Tantrism the disjunctions can be overcome, but in a way which itself has a sacred significance but at a higher level; perhaps it is better to say that sometimes the disjunctions are *suspended*. But as a crude simplification, we are not far wrong to say that the holy/unholy disjunction obtains, as the basic principle. The failure then to meet the conditions is equivalent to an infringement of them. By reasoning similar to that which we employed in the case of the chief, the blessing which might otherwise accrue to the worshipper becomes disaster. The fearsomeness of the numinous is now figured as wrath at the ungodly, to cite a Biblical way of speaking. (Hence the puzzlement when the wicked flourish; and the shattering effect of the Conquistadors' destruction of Inca images.)

Naturally, I am not concerned here to portray the situation in moral terms. The moral aspects of blessing and cursing, benefit and disaster depend on the way in which moral values are hooked up to the conception of the god. However, within a given framework of belief and myth, the judgement that the god brings disaster on those who do not fulfil the conditions, who are 'ungodly' in this sense, implies a certain acceptance of the conditions and an assumption of the relevantly beneficent power of the god in principle. The god is still the object of 'pro-' ritual. This is different from the situation of the anti-god and the appropriate anti-ritual.

The latter is a mirror image of the former situation, but obeying the same 'laws'. Under certain conditions of contact or intercourse, the maleficent power is going to be destructive. Apotropaic ritual (like making the sign of the Cross on the approach of the Devil) is a means of signalising and bringing about a lack of conformity to the nature of the Evil One, so that evil powers are not transferred.

It is now possible, in virtue of the foregoing rough and ready analysis of the basic behaviour of mythic divinities, to pick out certain themes found in myths. The point of this exercise is to indicate that the understanding of myth is not just a matter of story analysis (Lévi-Strauss' approach is thus too general [9]), but involves attention to the material content of myth, namely divinities. It is true that the nature of the divinities is very much determined by the materials to hand – I referred earlier to the *contingency* of mythic content in this respect. Nevertheless the contingencies fall within the framework through which the numinous operates.

First, looking at one side of the dialectic between a divinity and its worshippers, the concentration of numinosity in the divinity naturally leads, as we have seen, to the idea of a difference or a fixed gulf between it and the worshipper. This gap is often figured spatially, and helps to account for the differing levels of the cosmos to which we referred earlier. It is a recurrent theme in African mythology that once the sky was nearer, so that god was close to men, but that through

98

some transgression or accident the distance had been increased. The use of height to express superior power and status (note how the very word 'superior' incorporates the motif) makes the sky and mountains especially apt locations for divinities. But gods cannot get too distant, or at least not all the time, without becoming otiose. It is not just that men may cease to worship the distant being any more (the *deus otiosus* being as it were an ex-god), but that there is no occasion of his manifestation or presence among us, and part of this absence is indeed the lack of cultus. There must then remain, as typical, a continued transaction between the different heights or levels of existence. This is sometimes facilitated by the principle of likeness, so that an earthly god, such as Fire, can share in and manifest the power of the heavenly Sun (and in Vedic religion in the intermediate power of Indra's lightning): thus the earthly divinity can be identified with the heavenly one. It is sometimes facilitated by the recognition of a place as being especially the heavenly god's dwelling place, where his 'real presence' is most assured; similarly with sacred images, which signify the god and are in a sense part of him; likewise temporal 'places' can especially manifest the divine power. In all such cases the myths topically give an account of the god's special presence and indicate thereby the authorisation for regarding a place or time as holy or for regarding a particular rite or image as endowed with divine power. Since a rite can be indefinitely repeated in the appropriate conditions there remains assurance of the continued presence and power of the god.

Although distance is likely to be preserved between the worshipper and the divinity, the principle of likeness facilitates the identification of divinities themselves. To this extent the problem about polytheism is how it maintains itself. Part of the answer lies in the very fact that gods are cult- and place-related, so that the maintenance of special times and locations of special presence preserves distinctions. Another part of the answer is that by the same token different divinities can relate to different groups with their own specialised cults (consider the Greek divinities in this respect, and the caste and village related gods of India). Here it is often better to combine a kind of unity with diversity through myths of the origin of one

99

god through a superior one, for example by procreation. Still another part of the answer is that the powers of the gods are often mutually threatening and clashing. We may bring out some of these points by examining a myth described by Kees W. Bolle [10]).

At one time the world and the gods were threatened by a powerful demon. The demon was particularly hard to defeat since everything he put his hands on turned to ashes. It was Visnu who succeeded in destroying the demon by assuming the form of a beautiful woman, Mohini ('the deluding one'). The demon, infatuated, was asked by Mohini to anoint himself before coming to her. In anointing himself, he could not but touch himself, and thus he himself became ashes. While all this was taking place, Mohini had made a great impression on Siva. When the episode was over and calamity warded off, Siva asked Visnu to assume the same beautiful form. Aiyanar was born as the child of Siva and Visnu. The name Hariharaputra indicates this origin: 'son of Hari (Visnu) and Hara (Siva)'.

Aiyanar as a village deity of South India is related in this myth to the wider 'universal' tradition of the cult of Siva and Visnu. By being born of them he is, so to say, legitimised by them; or to put it another way, the cult of Aiyanar is legitimised in a broader (and as it happens Sanskritic) framework. He could, I suppose, in theory have been made to descend from *both* Visnu *and* Siva by putting their ancestry two generations back, rather than one (though then awkward problems arise about the superior status of the immediate parents). Given a one-generational gap between the two great gods and Aiyanar, the problem then arises as to how they can properly be his parents, seeing that they are both male. The transformation of Visnu into Mohini solves this problem, but for the solution to be satisfying there must be a reason for the transformation which connects up with Aiyanar's nature. This in fact occurs in the story, because Aiyanar's role is protective – he is a kind of divine village policeman and thus keeps the forces of chaos at bay.

100

The theme of a chaotic demonic threat to divine and world order is, of course, not infrequent in mythology. Put at its simplest the present myth incorporates the idea of a beneficent divinity, Visnu, and that of a maleficent adversary. Now the notion of Visnu's transformation and disguise is quite significant from the point-of-view of our present account of mythic forces.

Dealing with a dangerous and numinous force involves discriminating its nature so that appropriate action may be taken. The function of the chief's badges also, as we saw earlier, was to signalise his superiority over the person approaching him. Presumably if the maleficent demon were to recognise Visnu one of two things would have to happen: either the acknowledgement of Visnu's high status by the demon, a kind of defeat, or the presentation of a challenge. The latter would not be altogether favourable from Visnu's point-of-view as he would be liable to be worsted in any combat with such a sizzling divinity. Thus Visnu's power is best preserved by its being concealed through transformation. Visnu now instead of being apparently a threat to the demon becomes an alluring attraction. The tricky condition laid down by Mohini leads to an inversion. Visnu, really hostile to the demon, appears to be alluring; the demon seeming to be destructive of others is really destructive of himself.

The myth then combines a legitimation of a divinity by descent from superior divinities (and a similar legitimation of the cultus) and a story of clashing divine powers. The preservation of an atmosphere of conflict in the divine realm reflects the existential condition of men in a world where good, evil, and chaotic interplays of forces remain, however tidily and effectively different features of it are discriminated. Chaos also is the opposite of determinate creation. The creative power of divinity gives form to the world or to a particular aspect, and it is this determinacy which enables people to understand and recognise the conditions for dealing with divinity and with forces in the world. The chaotic is therefore a threat. Likewise transitional states where determinacy is lost come up frequently in myth as items of special significance. These in turn have an analogy to rites of passage, which signalise the proper transition from one condition to another.

Spirits of the dead, for example, may become threatening and demonic if their transition from this world into the next is not arranged properly.

Although a being of high numinosity shows its superiority and difference from the worshipper, so that there is an ontological dualism between god and man, a dualism which reaches its strongest expression in monotheistic cults, there are ways in which gods can possess and become powerfully present in human beings. Just as an image can be suitably endowed with the presence of its god, so can the priest and the prophet become similarly endowed. Some forms of divine kingship are of this character.

The main thesis which I have been advancing in this account of the dynamics of divinities is that the mythic–ritual milieu operates with its own principles of numinous power. But it by no means follows from this that it is possible to neglect other items of content. Clearly these are related to the circumstances of the mythmakers, for the very need for gods to show their power here and now, and again and again, give them very particular anchorages in the world. Similarly the dynamics will be affected by the structure of the society in which the myth-making occurs.

The fact that in this respect myths are like *collages*, assembling contingently given elements into patterns structured by the described dynamics, indicates the scope and limitation of psychological explanations of mythical motifs. It may be true to say that the *lingam* is a fertility symbol, and its disguised resemblance to an upright phallus echoes concretely the material that may be found in dreams. But this only indicates the manner in which this particular ritual item, the stone pillar, has been selected as a sign of the god's vivifying power. What is important is that it is taken as a sign. Since there can be very wide latitude in the perception of significant resemblances qualifying items to be signs, psychological explanations can sometimes throw light on why one thing rather than another has been selected. But they do not thereby explain the total structure or the type of dynamics involved.

The general account which I have given of mythic–ritual thinking can throw some light upon the hoary dispute about the difference between magic and religion. It is not a distinction which earns much respect these days, due to both the notorious difficulties besetting the definition of both terms and a better appreciation of the role of empirical beliefs and technologies among so-called 'primitive' folk. However, it remains the case that quite a lot of people in different manners perform rituals relevant to the success of practical enterprises and to the maintenance of the world order. These might be thought to be in some sense 'magical'. It would be simplistic to suppose, however, that the rites just bring about the result in question. (I leave aside here sorcery and witchcraft.) It would also be simplistic to neglect the relative nature of knowledge and belief; that is, the rationality of the ritual is related to the picture of the world and events held by the performers of the ritual. Given that a ritual itself realises the power of that towards which it is directed it can be seen as enhancing that power (for which reason gods are sometimes considered to feed on the sacrifices made to them, gaining substance from them). It also formalises the dependence of the performer and his group upon the god, so that it is as if there is a reciprocal recognition by the divinity of the group. These things being so, there *is* indeed a way in which ritual signs help nature on its way: man and the god form a cooperative system. But this is not to say that the ritual causes the coming of the rain. The rain god causes that (unless hindered by some other power), but the rain god's power has been recognised and enlarged through the ritual sign.

The ritual, then, forms but one part of practical activity in relation to the forces of the world. But in being a sign of those powers it draws men and their natural and supernatural environment into a single nexus. This is further reinforced by a consequence flowing from the nature of the ritual sign itself, namely that the occurrence of whatever may be wished for – the onset of rain, victory in battle, fearlessness – itself can be treated as a sign, as we say, 'Such-and-such is a sign of God's blessing.' Note that the very language here too is ritual, for blessing is the ritual release of beneficent power. Just as part of man's practical activities are specifically ritual, so the world acts both naturally and ritually.

It therefore would seem appropriate not to draw a line between religion and magic (all religions can be considered magical) but between differing kinds of religion. Thus some concentrate rather heavily upon fertility cults; others are primarily concerned with divine actions in history; some see blessings in this-worldly prosperity; others stress the acquisition of spiritual powers, and so on. These differing concerns will lead to very differing selections of the primary materials of the myths.

The preceding general account of myth has, of course, stressed its coordination with ritual, and it has also made considerable use of the idea of the numinous. It may therefore be of some interest to consider the role of mythic stories where the ritual and numinous elements in religion are not of ultimate importance. Here the religion of the Pali Canon of Theravada Buddhism may prove to be illuminating. For in this the ultimate aim is not salvation to be derived from a divine Being, but rather the stilling of those forces which make for rebirth, and the attainment of supreme peace and insight – such is the attainment of *nibbana*. And this end is not to be achieved by worship or sacrifice. Yet there are plenty of divinities referred to in the Pali canon; there are quite a number of encounters between the Buddha and the gods, while the drama of his transactions with the evil Mara are highly significant in his legendary life. The role of myth, consequently, is an ambiguous one in the Theravadin context. The teachings of Buddhism both play and fail to play in the same league as mythic thought.

Consider the question of the power of Mara [12]. He is the death-dealer, as his name implies, and he is death-dealer because he rules over and is identified with the sphere of sensual experience. Through pursuing the objects of sense we are bound ever more closely to the repetitive sequence of death, rebirth, death, and so on. Yet Mara is not at first sight simply a symbol of the sensual; that is, unlike Aphrodite in later poetry, a merely metaphorical concretisation of the forces of love. There is, as we shall see, an analogue of this in the case of Mara, but only at a certain level of exposition. In practice, Mara appears as the evil Tempter, liable to deflect even the Buddha from his chosen path. Yet he is defeated time and time again, both by the Buddha and by other *arahants* – the Buddha's victories, however, being prototypical. It is worth looking at the mechanism whereby Mara is defeated.

Basically, the weapon used is knowledge. The superior insight of the Buddha renders the blandishments and tricks of Mara vain. Of course, this knowledge or insight is not informational knowledge of an ordinary kind; rather it is insight into the underlying character of the world, attained existentially in meditative practice and buttressed by the serenity that self-control can bring. Thus Mara attempts to mislead by false teaching, for example, about the importance of severe austerity (which the Buddha had rejected) but he is reprimanded by the Buddha. He tries to disturb people's serenity, by for example making a loud noise while the Buddha is preaching to his disciples, but again the source of the noise is discriminated by the Buddha and overcome.

There are ways in which such stories conform to the mythic dynamics we have been discussed. First both the Buddha and Mara represent opposing threats, so that any occasion of encounter will lead to a dangerous transaction. Second, the power of the Buddha results from a combination of insight and serenity, and the opposed forces are delusion and sensuality. Let us consider the insight aspect. If Mara is to have any chance of victory he should try to escape its damaging power. Hence he tends to disguise himself (as a noise-making bullock, as a false-teaching brahmin, and so on) on his approach. It is appropriate for him to have this deceptive aspect, for more generally it is the deceptive appearance of things which binds men to the round of rebirth. His very power consists in deception. Thus his defeat is by the countervailing use of knowledge, signalised in the first instance by the fact that Mara despite his efforts at disguise is recognised by the Buddha.

In relation to conceptions of numinous power, the insight of the Buddha and of emancipated *arahants* thus appears as a superior power, yet it strictly does not belong to this realm of thinking. Likewise the Buddha himself can be called *devatideva* or 'god above gods', but he does not function in the Canon as a god. He transcends the gods, just as *nibbana* transcends all

105

heavenly regions, and the knowledge of *nibbana* all numinous powers. Thus the higher values of the Buddha's path have an ambiguous relation to the mythic–ritual realm. Though essentially playing in a higher and different league, they are to be viewed from the perspective of the religious milieu as super-powers. In so far as Mara exists as a summation of the threatening forces surrounding men, the teaching and insight of the Buddha exists as a superior force. But from the higher perspective Mara and the gods can be conjured away as empty symbolic figures. This comes out in the subtle transformation of the gods effected in Buddhist doctrine. The gods exist, as unseen psychological forces, but they are robbed of true respect. For they are categorised as impermanent, non-eternal, and thus not ultimately possessing the crucial property which is at the heart of salvation. They are as empty and without self as the empirical individual migrating from life to life. Ultimately therefore nothing is to be gained by cultivating them in worship and sacrifice, even if such practices are, within certain limits, tolerated in the Theravadin tradition. The transcendence of Mara and the gods has then to be seen as something more than the affirmation that something more 'powerful' than they exists (though this is in a manner true) and it could be for this reason that the Buddha condemned the display of *iddhis*, supernormal powers acquired by saints, for it would give the impression that the Buddha and his insight play in the same league, though higher up, as the gods and Mara. Rather, the heart of Buddhism belongs to a different order. It is therefore not in the last resort very surprising that the figure of Mara can be made to disappear in the analysis of the nature of existence, in the formal and more scholastic treatment of it in the *Abhidhamma*; Mara is, so to say, ultimately 'demythologised'. This, then, is the ambiguous status given to the mythic in the Theravada.

As matters developed, the Theravada was not of course without its rituals. Although the Buddha is no longer available for a true transaction, for the individual is as it were dissolved in *nibbana*, his popular prestige could yet be maintained in temples and ceremonies (not here true worship, yet overtones thereof) to signalise the Buddha's transcendence of the gods.

The monks' robes could too be the object of veneration, instilling some numinous power in the Sangha in a world suffused with such powers. Yet throughout the ambiguity remains, and these forms of cult are a skilful means to make men look beyond the numinous powers to the serene *Dhamma* which leads to liberation.

Is an explanation as to why Buddhism should display this ambiguous and ironic attitude towards the mythic–ritual world called for? At one level, of course, there is the fact that Buddhism was opposed to the highly developed sacrificial religion of the Brahmins. But though this was doubtless in a measure due to sociological motives, it is necessary to penetrate to the deeper reasons for the rejection (reasons which incidentally had some analogy to the rather different exercise undertaken in some of the leading *Upanisads*, namely that of reinterpreting the meaning of the sacrificial ritual in the light of the interior quest). The deeper reasons had to do with the psychological and contemplative character of the Buddhist path. Psychological, in that the doctrine of *karma* was interpreted primarily in terms of the attitudes and sentiments which lead to attachment and rebirth; contemplative, because the supreme liberation was to be achieved by a personal reorientation in the context of yogic techniques. *Sati* and *samadhi*, self-awareness and contemplation, represent the culminating elements in the Eightfold Path. However this contemplation was not directed at a god, an Other, as we find it in Sufism and in Christian mysticism: in brief, the locus of mystical knowledge had not received a prior definition as the Focus of worship and adoration, and as the supreme numinous Creator. Far from it; it makes no sense, in Theravada Buddhism, to speak of *nibbana* as the Focus of worship, and even the transcendental *Dhamma* which the Buddha realises in his life and preaching is only with a strain to be described as a *mysterium tremendum et fascinans*. *Fascinans*, perhaps, but in what sense is it *tremendum*, to be trembled in front of [13]? It is only from the ambiguous context of the transcendence of mythic powers that it would be possible to think of the *Dhamma* in this way. Thus the deeper reason for the true transcendence of the mythic and of ritual in Theravada Buddhism is that it ultimately

107

concentrates upon the contemplative experience as a means of liberation, without having previously defined the highest goal in terms of the numinous Object of worship and sacrifice. It exhibits therefore a style and atmosphere of liberation to which a numinous Focus is simply irrelevant. By the same token the dynamics of numinosity, as displayed in the realm of myth and ritual, are at best something to be taken into account in educating followers to go beyond their mythic–ritual milieu. Its Focus is beyond myth, transmythic.

There is a congruence between this approach to myth and the Theravadin treatment of cosmology. Thus the elaborate series of upper worlds, impermanent heavens, are correlated to differing stages of *jhana* or meditation. This equation between place and psychological state prepares the way for seeing the 'end of the world' (*nibbana*) as something to be 'seen' and 'tasted' by the saint at an even higher level of contemplative insight. At the same time full use is made folkloristically and mythically of the heavenly realms in exhibiting the previous locus of the Buddha before his descent to earth, the loci of the various types of gods and the rewards of good conduct, bringing one upwards towards the highest spirituality.

Having looked briefly at the place of myth in a religion which in certain respects transcends it, it is perhaps worth contemplating the mythic dimension of the Christian tradition, to illustrate a case where this type of thinking is very central, or at least has been traditionally.

At the heart of Christianity there is, of course, a doctrine of redemption and salvation. This ultimately involves a special interpretation of the myth of Adam. In his pristine state Adam is close to his maker, and though ontologically distinct, as is demanded by the unique holiness and creativity of God, he bears some analogical resemblance to him, and is singled out for special relationship to God. His powers are tainted, however, by the Fall, in which all men share, for Adam is the prototype and ultimate generator of mankind (even Eve derives from his substance). In a mysterious way Adam has failed to fulfil the right conditions for relationship with God. Thus God, though in principle beneficent, also is a kind of threat. The development of the conception of a single holy Lord in whom all

108

holiness whatsoever is concentrated (so that he is 'jealous' of the alleged existence of other gods) implies that any holiness to be acquired by man, to put him again into right relationship with God, must derive from God. The themes of Christ as the second Adam and as the Paschal sacrifice explain the Redemption, and in the following manner. First, by Adam death and the incapacity for eternal life (a crucial attribute of the divine Being) came into the world: a second Adam, taking on the substance and powers of humanity, enables men (by the principle of likeness) to share in eternal life. At the same time, secondly, the alienation of man from God due to man's transgression is overcome by a sign which easily outweighs the offence and thus averts the punishment of God, namely the sacrifice of Christ, on behalf of men. Solid with these themes is the argument: only God can save, only man can expiate, so God as man both expiates and saves. Only God can save, because it follows from the concentration of holiness, saving power, in one Being. Only man can expiate, since man is the source of his own alienation. But expiation, to be effective, must also involve an act of salvation, and hence the Incarnation.

But we may note further how the dynamics develop. Christ has to be considered as having two natures, partly because the ontological difference between man and God, required by the highly charged numinosity of a monotheistic faith, has to be maintained. Men can share in Christ's risen humanity but not strictly in his divinity. However, a lower analogue of the divine powers can be attained by man, though through the operation of God's grace and favour: he can rule his environment, cooperating thus with God's creative activity in bringing order out of nothingness; he can share in Christ's resurrection and thus be transfigured, he can have access to peace of spirit and love.

This 'transfer of powers' is altogether logical in terms of the mythic dynamics. The ontological difference follows from the limitless superiority of God as holy, and is reinforced by the ritual signs of that holiness including the praise and worship of God and the declaration by man of his own creaturely and sinful condition. These signs, incidentally, are given wider

109

extension by the recognition of moral attitudes, such as humility, and ethical conduct as forms of sacrifice and worship [14]. The ontological difference and the eminent status of God mean that there can be no automatic acquisition of divine powers through encounter (the attempt to manipulate encounters must therefore lead to divine counteraction). Any holiness must be transferred by God, and must fit the ontologically inferior condition of the recipient. This is the mainspring of the use of analogical predication in religion (though clearly there are other sources of it as well). The 'transfer of powers' also helps to explain the tendency for divine powers to become as it were semi-detached, as though for instance God's grace is a partly autonomous force. This tendency has, however, to be resisted from the point-of-view of the uniqueness of God's creativity and holiness, for no other source of holiness can exist side by side with it.

The historical events of Christ's life, death and resurrection provide a powerful myth, and through rituals it can be made present to men so that they can suitably participate in it – always bearing in mind that men cannot themselves become divine. We have already adverted to the re-presentation of Christ in the Eucharist, but other aspects of the story are equally illuminating. Thus the Christian participates in Christ's death. Just as paradoxically that death was a victory, so too with the Christian's initiation in baptism which is a kind of death towards sin, the 'old man' dies to be replaced by the new. Likewise the Christian can share by anticipation the power of Christ's resurrection. In being united with Christ, he gains the privilege of belonging to the harvest of which Christ is the first-fruit.

The dynamics also fits with the traditional roles assigned to the Devil. Given that a share in divine powers is conditional, and given further that holiness is given an explicitly ethical content, the failure to fulfil the conditions is a form of evil, to be treated as a challenge to God's power. Damnation vindicates God's goodness and maintains the *status quo* of his majesty, in a manner analogous to that of the chief. Since the Devil is the force hostile to God, and possessing evil rather than benign influence, it is paradoxically appropriate that he should be

God's agent of punishment. The evil person, in bearing a likeness to the Devil, is open to his influence and shares in his powers; these are the opposite of God's – notably the opposite of eternal life, or everlasting death. From a Christian point-of-view, however, there is no need ultimately to fear the Devil, despite his evil and threatening characteristics, for Christ's saving work is also figured as a victory over him. The Christian participates in that victory. This connects up with traditional apotropaic rituals. The sign of the cross is a sign of the power of Christ transferred to the Christian, which has superior force to the threatening opposite power of the Devil.

The dynamics of the Christian myth also shed light upon Satanism. Put crudely, we may say that God has two crucial constituent powers, holiness and goodness (for though numinosity does not have to be moralised, in the Judaeo-Christian case it very emphatically is). The sign of recognising God's holiness is above all worship. Hence the typical Christian response to the numinosity of the Devil is to try to ward it off, by a kind of anti-worship, such as cursing rather than blessing his name. But what if someone were actually to worship the Devil? One motive might be the identification of the Devil with some pristine God overthrown by the march of Christianity and now re-emerging in popular consciousness. Given the heavy identification of the Devil with evil and anti-social practices, the Devil-worshipper now uses evil (e.g., sexually orgiastic) practices as signs of acknowledgment of the Devil's power. From a mythic point-of-view this is quite intelligible, but it gives a special slant to Satanic revolts in a predominantly Christian culture. The other side of the coin is that it was quite natural for someone from a Christian culture to look upon the worship of some other god as being Devil-worship, given the premise that there are basically only two numinous beings, God and the Devil, and that the object of a people's cultus is numinous. This gives an extra edge to the iconoclasm liable to result from adherence to a 'jealous' monotheism.

The mythic dynamics also, of course, help to explain the logic of the Virgin Birth and Immaculate Conception. Admittedly the solution is not wholly tidy, but it is designed to account for the sinlessness of Christ, required by his divine holiness and also for his being a pure sacrificial sign of atonement. As such, sexual generation need not be regarded as evil (though the Church had its moments of so regarding it). More importantly it represented the prime transaction through which human powers are transmitted. In view of the sinfulness of Adam, sexual generation becomes the mechanism of transmission of sin. For Christ to be born of a human mother (necessary for his humanity) without sharing in the fallen state, the transmission has to be blocked (by the immaculate conception). For him to be divine, his origin is looked on as not wholly human (hence the virgin birth). The elevation of Mary to a high status in the cultus, such that there is suspicion from a phenomenological point-of-view that she is almost divine, represents the intuitive application of the logic of the mythic dynamics; Mary's immaculateness assimilates her to Christ. The difficulty of separating out clearly Christ's divine and human natures makes the *theotokos* title a secret lever for supposing that somehow the divine nature stems from her too.

One other aspect of the mythic–ritual dynamics of Christianity is worth commenting upon before we proceed to consider the ways in which the dynamics can come through into the doctrinalisation of the faith. We have earlier placed stress upon the re-presentation of Christ in the Eucharist, and have briefly adverted to the sacrament of baptism. The other great sacrament is preaching, and this involves some complex relationships between the use of language and the Holy Being to which it refers.

In view of the preceding analysis of the way in which signs work in the mythic–ritual context, as themselves exhibiting the power of which they are signs, and in view of the central place given to language in human, and more particularly ritual, transactions, it should occasion no special surprise that there should be a class of linguistic usages which are sacred. (Incidentally, the hidden sentiment behind quite a lot of contemporary discussions in the philosophy of religion, namely that there is some kind of a distinction between religious language and 'ordinary' language, is that there is a line between sacred and secular; but it should be recalled that wherever religion

112

is, ordinary religious language is quite as ordinary as any other uses of language.) That a use of language should be regarded as holy amounts, briefly, to the fact that it has a ritual employment in a transaction to do with holy power, and thus has somehow to bear signal characteristics of its affinity with holy power. By contrast 'profane' language (really blasphemous swearing) indicates its opposition to such an affinity. For this reason a purely 'intellectualist' approach to so-called religious language, that is, an approach not connecting truth-claims with the performative uses of language is hardly likely to be fruitful for analysis.

The sacramental character of preaching in the Christian tradition clearly owes much to the concept of prophecy, where the prophet acts as a vehicle of God's messages. A highly formalised and ritualised type of this vehicular transmission is already found in the institution of priesthood, insofar as sacred formulae derived from the divine Being are used in transactions with him. The characteristic of prophecy is the acquisition of the credentials for being an intermediary through a special kind of experience. More particularly, the prophet has a numinous experience, in which the Other irrupts into his consciousness. His words express this experience, and in so doing acquire a holy character. (I here leave on one side, for the sake of simplification, the question of the criteria that may be employed in a given culture for determining the validity of the prophetic claims: clearly there can be both hypocritical charismatics – those who falsely claim the experiential credentials – and misguided ones.)

It is partly in this tradition that we can understand preaching as a more spontaneous presentation of the reality of the holy Being than that available in fixed rites. Although preaching is not confined, obviously enough, to the liturgical context in Christianity, the distinction can be seen in the typical traditional liturgy. Whereas the form of the communion is relatively fixed, there is much more variation in sermons, a testimony to the attempt, even within a routine context, to preserve a spontaneity in the outpouring of the Word of God. Nevertheless the underlying dynamic is similar, hence the sacramental character of preaching.

This implies that in some form God is presented in the preaching. More particularly in Christianity the preaching has a salvific character, since the risen Christ is testified to. As with other sacraments there are conditions for the 'transfer' of Christ's power and in this respect preaching can also be seen as a kind of challenge. The response of faith, verbally acknowledged and presumedly free from hypocrisy, is a sign of the transfer of power. But the challenge may be rejected.

So much then for an outline of some of the principal features of mythic–ritual dynamics. These dynamics operate, of course, contextually and I have also emphasised the contingent nature of the items which may be taken up and woven into a mythic whole. And emphasis here should be laid upon the nature of the *whole*: to grasp the full implications of a sacred story one has to see not merely how it is coordinated to other sacred stories, but also how its items fit with a particular social structure, ritual institutions, and so on. One important cause of doctrinal reinterpretation of myth is the fact that a myth-bearing religion may make important cultural transitions, either out of one culture into another or out of one phase of a given culture into a different one. The transformation of the milieu will have an important bearing on the meaning of the myth. And it can often be that there is a tension between the assumptions of a myth and the state of knowledge of the culture into which it enters.

First let us consider a concrete case of milieu-transformation where an original myth is seen in the perspective of a synthetic religious movement which retains the older tradition in synthesis with an interest in a different kind of spirituality. I quote the following account of the Kabbalistic interpretation of the Fall [15]:

> The essence of sin is seen here in the disruption of the cosmic harmony, in the destruction of an original unity in which not only God's severity and grace were in a harmonious balance but in which all areas of creation itself were also permeated with this harmony and man stood in unbroken communion with God. This communion consisted in the contemplation of the divine and its mysteries, of the unity

114

of the living God which manifests itself in God's creative power. Adam's disobedience of the divine commandment was a decision which destroyed this communion and which was disastrous in its effect upon all creation. Sin produced separation where harmony and unity should reign: this is precisely its mysterious nature. 'Punishment' in the usage of the Kabbalists is the isolation of things and of man from God. Man who assimilated such isolation into his being and into his actions, creates a false, inauthentic view of reality ... This is developed in the Kabbalists' mystical exegeses of Adam's sin. The Tree of Life and the Tree of the Knowledge of Good and Evil are, according to the Kabbalists, fundamentally one ... Adam separated the trees from one another. He thus isolated the power, namely the principle of divine severity, which is operative in the Tree of the Knowledge of Good and Evil, and let it work upon him in isolation ... God's severity, his punitive justice, is now no longer restricted by the unbroken union with divine grace ...

This is not a matter of allegorising the myth. The Fall is retained as some kind of real event; nevertheless the myth is penetrated by concerns scarcely evident in the milieu of its origin. The clue to the new concerns lies, very clearly, in the emphasis upon contemplative union with God and of the harmonious unity of creation. These motifs bring out the mystical, that is to say contemplative, character of the Kabbala. The quest for the interior gnosis that will restore cosmic harmony is not, however, pursued in isolation from the older tradition. The numinous and the contemplative are here blended in a synthesis (one indeed which does not go so far as to see in contemplation a means of actually *becoming* God, an idea which would run counter to the dynamics of the numinous. Nevertheless one may note that there have been occasions upon which mystics have gone this far and in monotheistic contexts such claims do not, to put it mildly, make the orthodox happy, since in terms of the dynamics of the numinous they are indeed blasphemous). In brief the Kabbalistic aim is to retain the myth and in a sense add to it, as well as re-interpret it, so that it harmonises with these contemplative, mystical

115

concerns. In the new religious milieu the myth has undergone a transformation.

But transformation may also occur where it is the extra-religious milieu which has changed. A notable example is to be found in the post-Modernist Roman Catholic attempts to retain the story of Adam and Eve as being the ancestors of the human race, but now within an evolutionary framework (this leading also to the need to distinguish between physical and psychical evolution, the former being accepted but the latter not). The context now gives the story a very different flavour, and indeed makes the acceptance of the myth take on quite a new aspect compared with the way it was primordially accepted. For now a small hole has to be drilled in the fabric of scientific knowledge of the world to make room for assent to the myth. Such an operation was not originally in question.

The injection of a myth into a culture with a determinate world-view naturally involves the doctrinalisation of some at least of its elements. This process is much assisted by the fact that the very transition into another cultural milieu will raise questions of the true interpretation of the myth, for there is likely to be a confusion of interpretations resulting from the interaction of myth and milieu, especially if the myth-bearing religion aspires to universality and crosses many cultural divides. A prime example of the process was the evolution of doctrines to exhibit, in Greek and Latin terminology, the nature of the Christian God. Thus the Trinity doctrine succeeds well in systematising the nature of God as revealed in differing parts of the Christian mythic heritage, and it does so in a manner highly relevant to ritual (given monotheism, the existing worship of Christ *must* imply his full divinity and equality with the Father). Indeed doctrines, as systematisations and analyses of the constituents of divine and worldly reality, have to retain connection with the practical and experiential dimensions of religion if they are to retain their proper function.

Consider, for example, the idea of God's transcendence. This means, in one sense of transcendence at any rate, that God is 'beyond' the world. In the full context of God's creative

116

power, it means that the world depends upon something other than itself. However, this is not equivalent to saying that there is a First Cause from which the rest of entities flow or such that if it did not exist nothing else would (as C. B. Martin has observed, what if it were the Pole Star). The idea of God's transcendence still retains the notion of God's otherness from the universe, and it secretly implies that the world is as it were a screen behind which there lies the Transcendent. Such a conception is remarkably valid when it is related to the experience of God as the Other and when it is related to the mythic–ritual screening of the Holy. Thus the rather abstract-sounding doctrine of transcendence has connections with religious experience and practice.

Similar remarks can be made with equal, if not greater, force in regard to Theravada Buddhism. As we have seen, the mythic plays a transitional role here: the Buddha's *gnosis* transcends the mythic forces. But by this very token, the doctrinal analysis of reality has extreme importance. Consider the central role played by the doctrines of *dukkha, anatta*, and *anicca*. The analysis of reality therein given reflects that which the Buddha came to know experientially, in his Enlightenment. And a proper grasp of the nature of reality in the light of these doctrines is central to the process of liberation. The centre of the Buddha's saving work is then his promulgation of the teaching, the *Dhamma*. Now of course the *Dhamma* takes on metaphysical overtones, in that it can be regarded as fused with the transcendent state to which it points and as manifesting itself in the Buddha, as one whose true nature is unfathomable and transcendental. Nevertheless the *Dhamma* can be taken in quite an ordinary way as referring to the doctrinal teachings, together with their practical corollaries. Thus the doctrinal dimension of Theravada Buddhism is of peculiar importance.

Nevertheless it would be a misunderstanding to take the doctrines simply as metaphysical affirmations (though philosophical arguments may well be used to buttress them). For them to be 'effective' as part of the Buddha's saving teaching their import must be understood existentially and hence they are coordinated with meditative practices. Indeed in some respects the doctrines cannot be understood *apart* from the

117

practices going with them. This is notably so with the notion of the permanent 'place', the state of liberation, *nibbana*. One cannot make sense of this idea except in relation to the practice of techniques such as the *jhanas*. The goal is defined by the path leading to it. Hence the doctrinal dimension of Theravada Buddhism has even greater importance, and an even more directly existential character, than the doctrinal dimension of traditional Christianity. For very much at the heart of the latter is the myth of redemption, which the doctrines can only serve to interpret and clarify, while very much at the heart of the former is the experience of liberation from an existence known to have a certain doctrinally depicted character.

The classical Mahayana, it might be noted, transcends the mythic in a rather different manner by incorporating mythic–ritual ideas of salvation more directly into the fabric of Buddhist belief, while at the same time relegating all this to a lower level of 'everyday' truth which is superseded in the higher experience of the Void. The suffering, heroic Bodhisattva has power to save by transferring from his abundance of merit to the otherwise unworthy faithful, but both he and the celestial Buddhas disappear when one reaches the higher level.

Thus in general it is necessary to see both doctrines and myths as having practical and existential significance. The fact that this is so sometimes makes it possible for a kind of doctrinalisation to help in the retention of the values of a myth when the latter has been transformed into a symbolic or parabolic form. Thus in recent Christianity theologians have perforce been concerned to interpret the Adam myth somehow. That there were no such beings as Adam and Eve many Christians would now freely admit. But the story remains somehow authoritative. It does not matter that it is not literally true (yet when was it ever so: what counted as 'literal' when the story was first fashioned?). In this it becomes like a parable, for it matters not at all that there was no good Samaritan. It is then a story which signalises something about men's relationship to God – his continuing alienation from him and his disobedience. It thus is a story illustrating an existential relationship. Its inner meaning takes on a doctrinal rather than

118

a mythic guise, for it is about the structure of human–divine relationships. This is one manner of demythologising.

However, if the key concepts of the story are to be retained, notably the notion of *sin*, the presupposition of the numinosity of God must be retained also. (Of course, it is possible to go onwards in the direction of a highly radical demythologising in which even God's holiness is dispensed with, which means virtually substituting another description than *God* for ultimate reality: the question arising here is only whether such a stretching of the content of faith brings the Christian theologian to snapping point, an issue we discussed in an earlier chapter.) The retention of God's numinosity, as exhibited in ritual and in a certain kind of experience of God, gives the substitute for the washed-out myth a kind of homology with it. For though the myth collapses into symbolism and a parable, the dynamic of relationship between God and man is sustained, first by the affirmation of the reality of God doctrinally as transcendently *there*, and by the experientially vindicated attribution to him of holy power. Men here and now exist, even if the Adam in which all were thought to participate no longer does; and God exists, even if that particular transaction with primordial man vanishes into a parable. To this extent the major point of the original myth is retained.

This is one example of the effects of a new milieu on the understanding of a myth. It is worth noting that another option is open to the believer. He can, even in the face of evolutionary theory and the rest of our modern knowledge of prehistory, stick to the strict authenticity of the myth. Such a 'fundamentalism' however is even itself a new mode of belief, for the past did not demand such a sacrifice of the intellect, and the inner dynamics of the mind are bound to give a special flavour to the affirmation of the Adam story and thereby to its content. It is as though the surface security of such a faith requires a deeper hardness in combatting the threats to it. It is as though a modern literalness must be imposed upon the ancient material to prevent it from slipping from our grasp.

And this raises some deep questions about the ultimate viability of the phenomenological method. The attempt to be 'scientific' in the study of religion (for instance to discount the Adam and Eve story as an account of man's religious pre-history) appears to bring us into conflict with the substance of faith which is being described and explored. It is to this nest of problems that we turn in the next chapter.

4 Resolving the Tensions Between Religion and the Science of Religion

I have already made reference to the reflexive effect of Religion upon Theology. Since too there is an intersection between Religion and types of enquiry such as prehistory, history, archaeology, sociology, and so forth, as was exhibited in the first chapter, Religion is not an isolated pursuit. By the same token the Christian or other theologian is liable to feel the pressures of new knowledge upon his Expression of his faith. It is worth then considering how far there is liable to be a tension between actual religious belief, commitment, and practice, and the scientific study of religion. Here I think it is important to consider the matter from a logical or structural point of view. It is not of much concern here to consider the possible effects upon individuals of becoming devoted to Religion; from a religious and indeed also from an irreligious perspective the task of exploring or teaching Religion is a rather specialised vocation in which commitments frequently have to be suspended. But we are not specially concerned here with what sort of person is best fitted for such a peculiar occupation, or with what effects it may have upon him. Rather we are concerned with the question of how far the methods of phenomenological, historical, and sociological enquiry (etc.) yield results which are incompatible with various types of religious belief. As I hope ultimately to show there is no reason why the study of Religion should entail consequences hostile to religious belief. In the end its empathetic neutralism is preserved. Nevertheless it is clear that some scientific findings about religion will conflict with some beliefs. The aim of this essay is to sketch the limits of this conflict. This is more or less

121

to define the limits of religion as an autonomous phenomenon.

Let us begin with questions about the historical method, as applied to the New Testament material. This conveniently links up not only with the discussion in the last chapter of problems of the mythic, but also with our discussion of the status of the Focus in Chapter 2. The use of historical methods is, of course, tricky in connection with the Gospels, for so many questions about so-called 'presuppositions' enter. Hence my discussion must have the character of a rather simplified sketch.

At one level, the use of historical methods to probe the Gospels could be considered primarily a *technical* problem. If we are concerned with the question, for instance, of whether Jesus was sympathetic to the Zealots, there is not merely the problem of examining the evidence at a surface level, namely by combing the text for relevant items, but also that of assessing the evidence in depth, by asking what *kind* or *kinds* of documents we are dealing with, how far they aim to be biographical, how the traditions lying behind them were formed, and so forth. Though in principle the technical problem is isolatable from the others, in practice it becomes interwoven with Theological problems.

The technical problem is obviously highly relevant in one sort of enquiry which the Religionist might make, namely that of trying to penetrate to the religion of Jesus or of trying to discover the development of the religion about Jesus. It happens that these enquiries are also of considerable importance to the Theologian. Let us consider briefly why this is so. (This might seem a very naive question to ask: it is intendedly so, for it is thus that we get to first principles.)

The Christian Theologian will be interested in the religion of Jesus because of the assumption that the life (and death and resurrection) of Jesus is the supreme locus of revelation. Thus historical knowledge of Jesus will necessarily contribute to the proper delineation of the Focus of Christian faith. Now presumably, despite the Theologian's interest in Expressing, rather than merely describing, something about Jesus, he will (in so far as he is undertaking *historical* enquiry) not be importing Theological canons into his history-writing. It is perhaps difficult to maintain such a path of rectitude, especially

122

as, for instance, the doctrine of *sola fide* might make a high degree of scepticism about what can be known historically about Jesus attractive; or a certain kind of religious conservatism might drive one too much in the other direction. But in principle the historical enquiry is Theologically neutral. (I shall come shortly to the complication introduced into the argument by the belief in miracles.)

Assuming that the enquiry is Theologically neutral and in fact an item falling within the ambit of Religion, the question to be considered is: how far and in what ways can results of such an enquiry conflict with the Expression of Christian faith? Clearly the answer is heavily tied up with the varieties of Expression, which are so many, and so again I must repeat that this discussion must be a simplification.

Take a crude case. Suppose we discover that Jesus was a wanton murderer. This would be in intolerable tension with the doctrinal scheme through which the rest of the faith was Expressed. In a 'syllogism': God is good; the Son of God therefore is good; Jesus was bad: therefore Jesus was not the Son of God [2]. Again, suppose we conclude that Jesus never existed, then: the only way in which God can ever have saved men was through the death of his Son on the Cross; if there is a Son of God, it is Jesus; but Jesus did not exist: therefore God has not saved men.

As it happens, neither of these 'results' of historical enquiry is true or could ever in practice be established as true, but they incidentally indicate that traditional Christian faith is in an important sense falsifiable in principle. Naturally, the actual results of historical enquiry have a subtler relationship to orthodox pictures of the Focus. Here the question of ultimate conflict between faith and Religion turns on the degree of 'give' (the degree of elasticity) in the doctrinal scheme which expresses faith. For instance, consider the following 'syllogism': demons do not exist and psychic and other disorders cannot be explained demonologically; Jesus believed in demons; if Jesus was God he could not have had false beliefs: so Jesus was not God. Here the question is: is Christology flexible enough to allow that the Son of God could have had false beliefs? It is evident that most modern Theology has accepted that he

123

could, and indeed has tended to argue that Christ could not have been truly human unless he had been an 'historical' figure, that is, one who is in large measure culture-bound. Other moves are possible, of course: one can, for example, say that it is over-simple to say that demons do not exist – they were one way of conceptualising and categorising certain phenomena. Or again, there is the hard line: Jesus believed in demons, so there must be demons.

It seems that the Religionist is precluded from taking the hard line, but precisely why this is so must emerge later. So far, it would appear that the use of the historical method does not preclude some doctrinal schemes [2], though it appears to exclude others. The problem that should exercise us here is: how acceptable is it that Christology should be as flexible as is indicated above? This is partly returning to the problem of the gallery of pictures discussed in Chapter 2. But it is also opening up more generally a query as to the nature of the concepts, such as *Son of God*, used in the Expression of faith. If religious ideas, experiences, and so on, have their own dynamic and explanatory function, then their autonomy has a most peculiar air if the ideas are always in direct collision with historical explanations. This is not to say that they must contain truth, only that they have a certain looseness of texture. For to rule out in advance the possibility of some accommodation with historical conclusions appears to imply that their use has always been more than non-rational, but rather irrational.

It could be objected, however, that this argument is fallacious, for the concept of rationality is relative: what counts as rational or irrational belief is relative to the norms of belief in a given culture [3]. Thus it might turn out that whereas *now* (namely in the twentieth century) it is irrational to believe in an omniscient Son of God, for whom false belief would be an impossibility, it was not irrational in some earlier culture. And why? Because a previous culture had not self-consciously involved itself in the scientific pursuit of historical facts, and had left room for a kind of soft-headed 'fuzziness' where the hard questions about Christ's humanity had not been asked. There is obvious force in this point.

However, that there is a certain looseness of texture, as I have called it, in key religious concepts emerges from a number of considerations. First, the relation between the propositions of a doctrinal scheme (and its consequences) is largely not one of entailment [4]. Rather, one proposition or group may suggest some other. For example, that Christ rose from the dead suggests, but does not entail, that men's salvation will involve the resurrection of the body. Second, in the mythic–ritual complex, as we have seen, what counts as a sign (and what it counts as a sign of) is to do with relevant similarity or analogy, but this involves picking out some features to the neglect of others. Third, very often doctrinal exploration appears to consist of probing the myths and signs to see what can and what cannot appropriately be drawn out of them (by consequence a number of theological conclusions can look absurd, as is the case when a particular text is taken with literal and crazy seriousness, to justify, for instance, self-castration). All-in-all, the history of religions shows, for all the rigidities of tradition and orthodoxy, a surprising variety of interpretations and conclusions from a given authoritative deposit. It is almost as if there was a constant fight to resist the very looseness of texture which makes such variegation possible, a fight which stems from the need for authority and legitimation, and doubtless too from taking with some zeal the suggestion that since doctrines ultimately stem from the Eternal Being they must partake of well-defined everlasting validity.

Similarly of course with the sacred book. Part of the tension arising from the use of historical method upon the scriptures arises from the latter's liturgical and institutional status. (Hence the notion that the book itself participates in the eternal power of its Author.) This introduces two subtler ways in which there may be a conflict between Religion and Theological Expression of faith.

First, the liturgical, ritual character of the book is likely to give it properties not shared by a more straightforward historical narrative. Matthew, Mark, Luke, and John are thus a very different matter from Thucydides. This is one of the reasons, for all the changes which may have overcome its ritual use in the centuries since the early Church, why there is

125

a problem about wedding historical research to religious custom. In any event, the ritual aspect of the book marks it off as being in its particular way an Expression of faith. So the very use of scientific methods of investigation (however good, or inept, or pseudo-scientific, or penetrating) subtly creates a tension between its evidential use and its ritual use. Put crudely, the problem is: should one enquire into mysteries? By this is meant, of course, not that the deliverances of the book are necessarily impenetrable to human intellect (one, modern, sense of the word 'mysteries') though God himself may be so represented, but rather that the book is part of the fabric of religious and ritual action (the other sense of 'mysteries'). The air of brusque enquiry is not easy to mix with the atmosphere of adoration and communion. Here is a tension between criticism and piety. However, this tension is not one of utmost principle, though it is highly relevant in the sociology of knowledge as applied to religion. If it were to be characterised in logical or structural terms, it would be seen as a difference of method in approaching a certain body of written documents.

Second, the very character of the sacred book as having a liturgical (or at least a partly liturgical) function throws doubt, naturally, on its historical reliability; not necessarily because propagandistic points may be made in it, though this is possible, and not because necessarily there is any dishonesty in its being compiled, though this is conceivable. Both possibilities are doubtless to be probed by the historical method. Rather, the root of the uneasiness lies in the fact that the book may not be primarily interested in historical evidences, as we understand them. It may be rather uninterested in writing a biography, as we understand the term. Its interests, or spectrum of interests, may be far removed from those of the modern historian. Certainly they are rather far removed from the concerns of the present-day Religionist. These things being so, the documents must present an enigma and a host of problems. However, the main point is that they represent a doubtful basis for modern history and biography. Hence there can grow, often (one suspects) too luxuriantly, a scepticism, resulting most extremely in an agnosticism about Jesus scarcely reaching beyond the affirmation of his existence. For the rest,

126

there is the post-resurrection (post-what?) characterisation of the Lord.

This is an attitude not unparalleled in the modern treatment of other scriptures. The Koran, it is true, is too closely wedded to the person of Muhammad (which it is not *about*, in any case) to attract the same scepticism. But the Buddha was once a solar myth, and the Vedic hymns were a disease of language. It is to be confessed, on the other side, that almost certainly Lao-Tse never existed – a doing by non-doing which he would have appreciated, had he existed [5]. Part of the trouble lay of course in a Western, sort of Christian, supposition that the Truth, to be divine, must be historically real. But that is somewhat by the way, for though the same accent on historicity does not characterise all religions, the treatment of the Christian book remains instructive.

The scepticism which I described above represents a certain challenge to the orthodox faith, which again could be set out in a brief argument, a 'syllogism'. It is this: in order to love and to obey God, we must know what he is like, at least so far as it is relevant to our condition; the Christian God is revealed in the Old Testament, but more particularly in the New; God revealed himself there in Christ, who is Jesus, that is, he did if there is any truth in Christianity; but we know nothing about Jesus, beyond the fact that he existed; so there is no new revelation in the New Testament, and there cannot be any substantive truth in Christianity.

As usual such a neat argument can be resisted by denying a premise here, and questioning another there. It is possible, for instance, to resist the argument by still claiming that there is new revelation in the New Testament, but that it is found in the post-resurrection interpretation of Jesus in the primeval Church. This is, in its way, fair enough, but it rests upon two suppositions. First, that there was a resurrection which 'authorised' the primordial Church in its interpretation (which involved, let us not forget, the Eucharist, developing into its logical extension, the *worship* of the Lord). Second, that our ignorance about the historical Jesus is merely contingent, so that it is feasible (indeed actually the case) that somehow he justified in his life that congruence with the resurrection

127

experience which legitimised the titles subsequently ascribed to him, like *Son of God* and *Lord*.

The first supposition, of course, is the one which is most charged with problems. The second is feasible, but would scarcely make sense without the first. In order to come to grips with these subtler tensions between Religion and Theology, let us turn aside for a moment to consider what might be said from a phenomenological point-of-view, for all too often the notion of what counts as historical evidence is concerned with the 'outer' events, while equally too often the phenomenological exercise is mixed up with the presentation of what is sometimes called the Theology of the New Testament (I use the capital 'T', for in this context, for the most part, the Theology is endorsed, authoritative indeed). Let us then briefly look at the resurrection from the point-of-view of the early Church, not so much with regard to the controversial details of the different accounts, but more with regard to what in principle appears to have been believed.

First it was believed that Jesus appeared to various people, and in a somewhat mysterious way, being, so to say, both recognised and not recognised (consider the road to Emmaus). Second, this reappearance of Jesus after his crucifixion was believed to be a datum of great significance for understanding his messiahship, that is, the experiences of the disciples and others (or what were believed to be their experiences) received an incipient interpretation in terms of the tradition out of which Jesus had come. Third, from an historical point-of-view it is baffling to know what to make of the circumstantial but not very consistent accounts of the risen Christ; but it is clear that as risen he was Focus of the faith of the early Church. Where there is a greater clarity, it is in the description of Paul's conversion (though even here the description is somewhat exiguous). In this matter it is clear that for Paul a numinosity surrounded the figure of Jesus. Thus we can say that as a Focus of faith Jesus indeed transcended his earthly existence and yet the details, or rather some of the details, of his life were prized in the tradition. Or again more precisely, what were believed to be some of the details were prized. In short, the logic of the early Church's attitude to the risen Christ pointed them back

128

to the figure of Jesus, who walked and talked with men. A substantive part of the myth of Christ was his earthly ministry (as it is later called). Phenomenologically, therefore, it is scarcely possible, however dubitable the liturgically oriented records may be, to divorce the risen Christ from the man Jesus, as far as the early Church was concerned. The radical modern scepticism about the historical Jesus must then represent some break with the records themselves. As, however, I have pointed out earlier, there is no reason why there should not be a kind of continuity in divergence, and yet the question arises as to the degree of tension between datum and interpretation (the N.T. and Theology, for instance) which can be tolerated in a continuing religious system. Thus the highly sceptical position is one of great tension, though presumably it cannot be ruled out as a possible development of Christianity.

So far we have explored, rather crudely, questions of the compatibility of doctrinal schemes and the use of the historical method. Yet little has so far been said about *explanation*. For a Theology may attempt to incorporate some sort of explanation of events; for example, the success of the early Church in establishing itself and carrying on the work of Christ was due to God's power working in men. Is there not here bound to be a clash between a naturalistically oriented approach and one which seemingly appeals to the supernatural? Before trying to answer this question, let us first clear out of the way some respects in which Religion is bound to affect Theological judgement.

First, if it were established that there were close parallels between (say) the religious experience of Paul and that of the adherents of some other faith, and if Theologically Paul's experience is deemed revelatory, then there is a presumption of revelation in the other faith. One can only so far say 'a presumption', for there might be other factors to be taken into account [6]. However, from a logical point of view such parallels yielded by comparative study would have to be taken seriously by the Christian Theologian. This is one reason why the comparative study of religion is viewed with a certain caginess by some Theologians. To one kind of Theology, highly exclusive, it can be a threat (though it should also be said that sometimes an over-enthusiasm for parallels can itself stem from another sort of underlying Theology – it is necessary for such presuppositions to be brought to the light).

Another respect in which Religion may affect Theological judgement is, obviously enough, in the use of the results of historical results in the description of the detailed mode in which God's power is supposedly operative, for example, through piecing together the debates concerning circumcision, etc., in the early Church. Indeed a great deal of what occurs as New Testament studies has as its aim the throwing of light on the substance and mode of God's activities. (This is not to say that at the same time it cannot be 'objective' history.)

However, let us look now more generally at the proposition that the growth of early Christianity was due to God's activity. Is such an explanation incompatible with a straight historical explanation? Suppose, for example, that appeal is made to miraculous events as caused by God, and as contributing substantially to the process of establishing the Christian faith.

Here we are in well-trodden territory, but some remarks on the philosophy of miracles are in order. The bite of Hume's well-known essay is concerned less with what might or might not have happened in the way of extraordinary events as with the assumptions that the investigating historian needs to make. As far as the logic of science goes, a unique 'sport' in the flow of events is compatible with adherence to the scientific method [7]. It is not therefore possible *a priori* to rule out the 'sport'. Of course, in the classical definition of a miracle, a miracle has to be more than a 'sport'. It has also to be caused by God, and so must bear some mark of this. (This links up with the idea of the miracle as a 'sign' in the New Testament.) It is also true that extraordinary events, not fitting in with the rest of experience and happening in a divinity-related context, do occur. Thus there are undoubtedly some strange healings at Lourdes, and this is in a divinity-related context. What, then, would be absurd about a Theological explanation incorporating reference to miracles (for example, the impetus given to the early Church by the miraculous events at Pentecost)? And why should such an explanation be resisted by the sensitive historian?

Superficially, the answer could be put in a 'syllogism':

educated men nowadays do not believe in miracles; the historian is an educated man; therefore when a miraculous event is described in a text, the historian must treat it as a false description. But this would be to represent the matter as one of ideology, which is the prevailing climate of assumptions among the aristocracy of learning, and it would be easy enough for the Theologian to mount a counter-ideological attack. ('It all depends on your presuppositions, my friend'.) The logic has to go deeper.

It can be simplified thus: not all stories about supposed events are to be believed; it is therefore necessary for the historian to sift the true from the false; thus he must ask by what test one should accept the descriptions of unprecedented types of events (for example, turning water into wine). One stylised answer will break down, namely: where the records are of divine origin, they can be trusted. For this would simply be to withdraw them altogether from historical scrutiny.

The search for a test is greatly bound up with probing, from a scientific point-of-view, the development of a tradition in which miracle-stories find their place. For a story may occur either because the events, roughly as described, occurred, or because the context is one where such stories are generated and attached to the principal actor or actors in the drama. It is doubtful whether a fully articulated and satisfactory theory of the development of miracle-stories is available. But a sketch is possible, for to some extent the process of welding traditions together will have involved a type of mythic inference (if he was the Son of God then such-and-such, e.g., the Virgin Birth, must have been so). It is not a question of dishonesty or simple propaganda, but rather the attempt to get the *collage* right. The tradition in this sense will 'obey its own logic'. But if one adopts such a theory to deal with at least part of the miraculous, it does not exhaust the matter or permit one, as an historian, to be simply naturalistic. As to why this is so we shall come back to in a moment.

But to interpose a point about the limits of a theory of miracles. It might be supposed that some special explanation is required if stories are generated which do not correspond to the facts. Suppose Jesus did not turn water into wine, then how

131

is it that soon people began to say that he had? Maybe a parable has become miscategorised, or a fragment of dialogue given, so to say, the wrong context and commentary. But no such special explanation is required in relation to those who *receive* such stories in good faith. That is, the picture of the Focus (Christ) held in say the second century A.D., including the miraculous details, can be fully in accord with the style of thinking of the times, and in no sense especially incongruous. The sceptical historian would be greatly mistaken if he imported his own rationalism, or his theory of the genesis of the miracle-stories, into the later context. The II-picture is now 'given', and with it part of the fabric of the life of the continuing Church, which itself is a force within society. As it were, the miracle-stories now have their own autonomy and power, and the reality of what they declare is projected onto the Focus. Put another way, it is partly through *them* that the Focus works.

I said a little while back that a theory of the genesis of miracle stories does not impel the historian to be straightforwardly naturalistic. For, to put the matter aphoristically, it is the supernatural aspect of the Focus which attracts the stories to it. Further we cannot always be sure that the miracle-stories are not based on particular manifestations of the supernatural. (Actually, though I use the contrast 'natural' and 'supernatural' here, it is not in an altogether serious way – the contrast needs transcending or replacing.) The general point being made here can be explained, a little circuitously, by reference to Paul's conversion on the Damascus road.

That Paul had a dramatic experience is, I presume, not in doubt. That he regarded the Focus of his experience as being Christ is also presumably not in doubt. That Paul's life was radically altered by the experience is again not in doubt, and it formed the basis of his legitimation as an apostle, for he too saw the risen Christ. There is nothing historically inconceivable about the inrush of like experiences upon the other apostles to form the core of what was meant by the Resurrection. The story of the Transfiguration (itself possibly a misplaced Resurrection narrative) also testified to Christ's numinosity, his appearing to men as a divinity, beside his earthly career as

132

a man. An historical explanation of the rise and spread of early Christianity would have to take the power of such experiences into account. That power is further conveyed, one might say, in the continuing and developing rituals of the Church, where the risen Christ is the Focus of adoration.

The numinosity of Christ itself is relevant to the attraction to this Focus of miracle-stories. If he was Son of God, it was quite 'natural' that he should have power over storms and that he should have been heralded by angels. And presumably the man Jesus did have healing powers. At any rate, for the projection of the risen Christ onto the man Jesus it is reasonable to suppose that the disciples were able to look back at Jesus as a charismatic figure, with mysterious authority. Proceeding in a quite understandable manner the makers of the tradition mounted a *collage* of which Jesus was the central piece. To understand his role and his manner of saving men and his risen numinosity, various conceptual materials lying to hand, Messiahship and resurrection of the dead, were bent into place. But the mythic–ritual *collage* had to proceed with what was given. Jesus was crucified, for instance, and sense had to be made of that. Such, then, might be a theory of the genesis of the incipient myth and Theology of the Church.

But to return to Paul. Did Christ really appear to him? That is, was it really God who brought about his conversion, and impinged thus dramatically upon his consciousness? If it was, then in an important sense the rise of the early Church was due to the power of God, for here was God's power setting Paul on the path which led to the wide diffusion of the Gospel through his missionary activities. And by parity of reasoning, one supposes that whenever God impinged on Paul's consciousness – frequently in prayer, for example – he, God, was a factor in the spread of the Church. And whenever the Lord's Supper gave men power to suffer and to gain peace, it was God working. If we accept all this, then how trivial did the earlier discussion of the miraculous appear! Not so very much difference is made by turning water into wine for the sake of a wedding-feast. How much more powerful is the constant pressure of God as Focus of men's religious and daily experience!

It might be said on the other side that all this was a sort of illusion. Paul thought it was Christ there on the Damascus Road, But it was just a nervous crisis that he had, and he connected its effects with Jesus. Men *think* they encounter God in prayer, or at the Lord's Supper, but this is merely fancy. There is no one there really. So it would be rather ridiculous to say that God's power works so strongly in the determination of historical events.

It is curious that two such different slants could be put upon the same set of events. How is one to choose between them?

It is often good advice to pause before rushing into a disjunction. What sort of choice is being asked for? By what criteria would one determine whether or not it was Christ that Paul encountered on the Damascus road?

This is an area where philosophy of religion becomes immediately relevant to questions of scientific enquiry; not in the sense that all problems of methodology are in a manner philosophical, but more directly because issues about tests of truth in Theology enter in. They enter in because the judgement that it was indeed Christ who encountered Paul on the Damascus road is a Theological affirmation. And contrariwise it is important to investigate the grounds of scepticism about this Theological affirmation, as represented by such statements as 'It was just a nervous crisis which Paul had'. Again: undoubtedly Paul had an experience of some kind but what are the grounds for identifying its Focus with Jesus and the risen Christ? To say that Paul was suffering from some illusion presupposes that one can tell illusion from reality in this area. Again, we are treading into the territory of criteria of truth. Issues become indeed complicated because no straightforward appeal to empirical tests can be made, since the sense of 'empirical' in effect shifts from one culture to another. How then are we to proceed?

We must first notice a distinction. If we consider Paul's experience, it may be considered 'valid', to use the common, rather odd jargon, on at least two different bases. First it may be considered valid on the ground that it is an experience of God (ultimate reality, etc.); or better, that it is itself a legitimate ground for believing in some transcendent Being. The words are rather vague but they are meant to be. The first

134

sense of validity has to do with the general import of the experience. Second, Paul's conversion may be 'valid' inasmuch as it is genuinely an experience of the risen Christ. Here we come to the particular. Doubtless the second validity depends upon the first, for if there were no transcendent Being then the risen Christ would not manifest it. (Still in principle we might keep another option open: a non-divine, non-transcendent risen Christ, perhaps after the mode of Paul van Buren [8]; yet it may be reasonable to neglect this possibility in the present discussion.)

Very roughly, the first kind of validity is to do with the general, root question as to whether religious experience should be trusted for what it in general testifies to. In mind here is such a treatment as Otto's 'The Idea of the Holy'. Though it is highly doubtful whether his concept of the numinous experience can be made to run the whole gamut of religious experience (indeed in my view there are some main sorts of religious experience, of which perhaps the major, but certainly not the only, one is the numinous experience), yet numinosity has a sufficiently wide range to make us ask whether this kind of experience is somehow verifiable. So to simplify the operation, and leaving aside other major categories of religious experience such as the mystical or the contemplative, let us look upon the general question, à propos of Paul's conversion (assuming it to be a type of numinous experience), as this: does Paul's experience, as an instance of a type, have validity as being an experience of the Transcendent?

Why should it not? Here structural and dialectical issues may become important, as described in Chapter 1. For the general question of the 'validity' of the numinous experience may well lead us into psychological theories, the reason being that they may provide explanations of such experiences of a sort to lead us to doubt their 'validity'. Of that more later, but let us assume for the time being that there is no specially compelling reason to doubt the general 'validity' of Paul's experience; what nevertheless has to be said about the particular claim that it was genuinely an experience of the risen Christ?

The criteria here have scarcely been explored in recent

135

times, and in ancient times they have been intuitive or unconscious, not brought to the surface of enquiry. One can hazard the secret, unconscious considerations that might make Paul's claim that he had experienced Christ intuitively convincing: the fact that it seemed to him that it was Christ; the fact of his being a changed person; the later fruitfulness of his mission; his grasp of the meaning of Christ (here some non-vicious circularity of thinking might enter in); the consonance of Paul's preaching with that of the other apostles, despite tensions; the general acceptability of his experience as being of a divinity, and so forth. These grounds cannot *a priori* be judged absurd or the reverse. But what other signs and marks would be required of the validity of Paul's particular claim? The tests of identity of the object experience and Focus of the traditional faith are never cut and dried, and how could they be? It is hard to see how on the basis of the scientific study, Religion, it is possible to refute the Pauline claim; nor is it possible in these terms to confirm it conclusively. Thus, leaving aside the question of the *general* validity of religious experience, the 'scientific' judgement on Paul's identification of the object of his experience with Christ must remain agnostic. It follows that the historian, again within the limits laid down in this argument, should be agnostic.

But he is not agnostic on the *power* of Paul's experience, for that enters in strongly into the explanation of the spread of the early Church (likewise with the largely undocumented experiences of the faithful, also doubtless oriented on the same Focus, namely Christ). In brief, the historian has to look upon the matter phenomenologically. The Focus (bracketed) entered into Paul's experience and was a prime factor in the spread of the Gospel. All this can be said without uttering from a Theological standpoint or from the standpoint of naturalistic atheism. This was part of what I meant by saying that it is necessary to take the supernatural into account.

To this extent the Religionist's (or historian's) account is compatible with the Theological Expression of faith, namely that it was through the power of God that early Christianity was established. Though compatible, however, it differs from the Theologian's description. The historian is not uttering any kind of faith statement: he is not, *qua* historian, speaking as a Christian. Rather he is accepting a phenomenological description of the Focus of Paul's experience, and recognising that Paul's actions were highly influenced by what he (Paul) took to be the object of his experience. The historian is also recognising that such an experience has its own validity as power, as a force (to put it crudely) in the determination of the affairs of mankind. Yet a few mysteries remain on the other side. What is the Theologian affirming beyond what the Religionist historian can aver?

He is of course endorsing the correctness of Paul's own affirmation of faith. But in saying that it was through God's power that the Church came to be established he is saying something quite on a par with the Religionist's judgement, or so it would seem. But of course it is vital to look to the context. The Theologian makes the claim in the context of piety (God is to be praised for establishing the Church) and God's action is seen as part of the continuing drama (or myth) of salvation history. The Religionist on the other hand is not directly Expressing any faith or affirming the reality of salvation.

All of this part of the discussion has been predicated on the assumption of the possible general 'validity' of such experiences as Paul's. It is now time to turn to this broader issue left on the agenda. It is an issue which falls within the bracket of what we called, in Chapter 1, phenomenological–dialectical studies of an aspectual sort, and it belongs in principle to the psychology of religion. However, the problems raised present a philosophical face also.

A major element in the discussion concerns, obviously enough, the role of psychological theories as explaining such an experience as Paul's. More particularly, can such an experience be 'explained away' as, for example, 'just a nervous crisis', to quote my earlier crude characterisation of such an explanation? And what is meant by explaining *away*?

The importance of this last question is evident from a curious fact, or rather from a range of curious facts. In the context of theism, for example, the existence of a Creator on whom all things (and all sequences of events) are ultimately dependent gives a strange twist to any claim to explain a conversion in terms of previous psychological and other events. The fact that a conversion is so explicable appears compatible with the belief that it is in some sense brought about by God. For whatever the causes and occasions of the conversion, the causes and occasions are divinely ordained and caused. I shall in a moment be more explicit about this point, but in the meantime it is worth noting that similar arguments can be employed in relation to some non-theistic systems, for example, to those where there is belief in *karma* and rebirth; for at the metaphysical level the determination of events in a karmic manner can play a like role to that occupied by the Creator in the theistic case. I am not of course saying that *karma* is Creator. Obviously it is not, for it is a concept of quite a different order. But in relation to supposed psychological and other explanations referring to previous causes of a conversion (or Enlightenment, the attaining of *nibbana* and so forth) the doctrine of karma can play a similar part: for it is not due (somehow) to Karma that the prior occasions and causes of Enlightenment (or whatever) have come to pass? This is an argument exploited by, among others, McTaggart [9].

What, then, could be meant by saying that something is 'explained away'? Crudely, the notion seems to amount to this: that whereas the Christian Theologian explains a range of experiences as being due to the action of God upon individuals, the (or rather *a*) psychologist presents an alternative and better explanation. The previous remarks about the apparent compatibility of the God-explanation with the psychological one were meant to indicate that *prima facie* the two kinds of explanation are not *alternatives*. If this were so, then how would the question of one being better than the other relevantly arise?

It could arise if one of the two explanations E1 and E2 which are compatible is unnecessary. Suppose that E1 is better than E2 and one is unnecessary, then it would be rational to use E1 and to dispense with E2. Naturally there are questions, which I shall come to, as to why one explanation should be regarded as 'better'. In other words, there are problems of the criteria of power, fruitfulness, and the like of explanations.

These remarks seem to indicate that there is already an

138

issue arising about the very idea of two compatible explanations. For surely, if E1 is a good explanation it explains sufficiently why the event (e.g., a conversion-experience) occurred; in this case E2 has a peculiar role. What can it explain if E1 has already sufficiently explained the event? Or to put the matter in another way: if E2 does any explaining at all then it at least partly (even if not necessarily sufficiently) explains why a given event occurs. But if it does *this*, then how can E1 *sufficiently* explain the phenomenon in question? It would appear that for E1 and E2 to be compatible explanations they have to be *joint* explanations. Consider, for instance, the once fashionable distinction between reasons and causes (of human action): should this not have implied that the reasons and causes had to be taken *together* to account for a person doing X rather than Y? [10].

Most importantly the discussion raises the following issue: is the explanation of a religious type of event (e.g., a conversion-experience) by reference to a transcendental factor, such as God, *necessary*? Does it not remain a superfluous comment, perhaps even just a kind of expressive value judgement? For if we suppose that psychological theories can account for conversions, then they represent a sufficient explanation of them. In this case the talk about God bringing them about is simply superfluous, as explanation.

Of course, it is only a supposition that psychological theories can deliver the goods as indicated above. It is undoubtedly a matter of dispute as to whether any particular psychological theory of religion and of conversion-experiences in particular is sound. My own view, which I do not argue here but which I have sketched elsewhere, is that the present theories are rather poor from an explanatory point-of-view, partly because of the relative ignorance (an understandable ignorance, however, in view of the intellectual milieux in which their authors have been trained) of the facts about religion. For instance, Freudian psychoanalysis is largely based on a very narrow survey of the facts, not to mention some unsupported speculations about religious origins and so forth. For it is an elementary observation that a psychological theory about the genesis of religious sentiments, symbols, and ideas needs to be wide-ranging and

139

based upon the evidence of different cultures. Unfortunately these evidences have not generally been available to those with medical and psychological training. Or if one may be a little naughty: psychoanalytic approaches to religion have gained their practical success from intensifying certain attitudes found genuinely in a section of the Victorian and post-Victorian bourgeoisie. But this apart, for what it is worth, it is plain that the psychologist and psychoanalyst has little experience of the data provided by Religion. Even Jung, who ranged widely in Asian and other traditions, was harvesting a crop of symbolism determined greatly by his own metaphysics. In brief, it cannot as yet be said that psychology or psychoanalysis has provided a satisfactory theory of the genesis of religion. But so what?

It is no criticism of a science that its answers are as yet patchy and feeble. The chief questions are: does the science in view hold promise? Is it likely to be fruitful? What can it establish *in principle*? We therefore have a different dimension added to the supposition that psychological theories might, as we have said, deliver the goods. It is not what they can do now that is important; it is what they might do in the long run. Even if they can do little now, they might do a lot for the future. Thus a (say Christian) Theological account of religious experience, for example, conversion-experiences like Paul's, might attract a kind of long-term superfluousness, in view of the open-ended potentialities of psychological investigation.

It is now time to step back a moment and to consider what difference is made by introducing the third way between, so to say, the supernaturalistic and the naturalistic explanations, namely the possibility of phenomenological enquiry. Is it possible to speak of a *phenomenological* explanation of such experiences?

In a very limited sense of explanation, it is at once obvious that one can: for at a very low level the mere comparison of one man's experience with another and the typing of them together as two instances of the same type represents a kind of explanation. But our question is rather a different one, and certainly a deeper one. It turns, if you like, on the question of whether religious experience has its own kind of autonomy. Is there an experience of the Holy, for example, which is just

140

one of the 'facts of life', like seeing colours or discriminating musical forms? If so then the human environment has to be considered as containing a religious aspect, to which some people are, so to say, sensitive. In this case, it might be that the question 'Why do people have conversion-experiences?' cannot be solved by psychology alone, just as the question 'Why do people sometimes see trees?' cannot be so answered. After all, people see trees because trees are there to be seen.

Unfortunately the status of the assertion that the environment contains a religious aspect, namely the Holy, is unclear. Certainly it can be admitted by anybody (I think it *has* to be admitted by anybody) that numinous experiences occur. Men have visions of the Other. But to say that the universe contains in its substance an aspect called the Holy might be taken to amount to the claim that the phenomenological object or objects of numinous experiences actually exist(s). It thus becomes an existence claim. But such an existence claim seems to be but a generalised Theological claim, a kind of vaguer affirmation of the existence of God. Certainly this is the impression conveyed – quite deliberately in the context in which he was writing – by Rudolf Otto in his 'The Idea of the Holy'. He was deliberately driving a post-Schleiermacher wedge into Kant's distinction between natural science and morality. It thus appears that what was represented above as a 'phenomenological' kind of explanation turns out to be a disguised Theology. What then could be meant by the idea of the 'autonomy' of religious experience, an idea to which I referred a short while ago?

In view of the previous discussion about the status of supposedly alternative explanations, which really must serve as *joint* ones, the 'autonomy' of religious experience should imply that some explanation of a religious experience has to occur jointly with a psychological one in accounting for it. But if it is to be a kind of phenomenological autonomy, this explanation should itself be 'bracketed', and should thus not be a Theological one. It is hard, however, to know what sense to make of such a suggestion. To get at what it might mean, let us revert briefly to the question of the status of a Theological explanation of a conversion-experience.

141

A Theological explanation, crudely, is something like this: that such experiences are brought about by God; or at least part of their explanation is that God is *there* to be perceived (just as nirvana might be 'there' to be experienced). To call such a claim an explanation is grounded upon two factors. First, the existence claim ('It was God whom he saw', implying that there is a God) gives a ground for not being too surprised that such experiences recur, just as we are not surprised that men in different cultures see the moon. Second, doctrinal schemes, in which the concept *God* occurs though in differently ramified ways, can connect a given type of experience to other facets of the world and of history. Thus to say that God brings about conversion-experiences is to link the latter up with certain other patterns of behaviour, such as moral action and so on. We might briefly call these two kinds of explanations respectively existence- and connection-explanations.

Now given the empathetic neutrality of the phenomenological approach, a straight existence–explanation is ruled out. That is, the phenomenologist is not in a position to say *tout court* that a type of experience occurs because God or nirvana is 'there' to be seen. And the lesser claim that there are 'phenomenological objects' of such experiences does not amount to an existence claim in the required sense. Thus as far as this side of the matter goes, the phenomenologist may have to content himself with the lowest level explanation (referred to earlier), that there are well-attested types of religious experience, and to this extent the fact that a given individual has one is no tremendous occasion of surprise. But although this may so far sound rather a modest or even trivial claim, it may be of some importance nevertheless. For it indicates that certain general patterns occur, which themselves may have powerful effects (for after all conversion-experiences, for example, often do so); and it raises the problem of their explanation. It is quite beyond the state of present evidence and theory to say that their occurrence can be explained by reference to other non-religious factors. Whether they will be so in the future depends on the future. After all, a project of reductionist psychology (to which we will come later) may break down, and the existence of religious experiences may itself give shape to a new

142

psychology beyond anything that we so far have dreamed of.

As for connection-explanations, it is clearly possible for the Religionist to point to internal structural explanations, for example the connection between the *bhakti*-type experience and doctrines of grace (or its analogues). It is a fair enough presumption that *bhakti* generates such doctrines (rather than the main onus being the other way round). Likewise it is not unreasonable to connect a certain pattern of yogic training with a type of mystical experience. The one in some sense brings about the other. These examples indicate an inner-structural dynamic within religious phenomena which it is highly doubtful whether a reductionist psychology (or sociology) could neglect. To this extent also there is an autonomy in religion.

One can here make an analogy with music. Certain developments in music have to be understood by reference to creative attempts to use the tradition and go beyond it. To understand Beethoven one needs to understand something of Mozart. Obviously the psychology of a composer is quite important; obviously also a sociology of music can bring meritorious insights. But the stuff of music, its 'logic', has to be brought in fairly centrally. Likewise the psychology of Bonhoeffer, his social and political predicament in Nazi Germany, all these are highly relevant. So too was his own perception of his mission, against the theological tradition which he developed in his own idiosyncratic manner.

I have used the phrase 'reductionist psychology', and this certainly needs explication in this context. Strictly it is to be distinguished from something rather like it, which I shall deal with briefly first, and which I may call 'deflationary psychology' (similarly 'deflationary sociology'). It was once fashionable among Christian propagandists to ascribe Muhammad's prophetic experiences to epilepsy. Suppose we had a generalised version of this thesis, namely that all prophets are epileptics. Now it is true that technically one might argue that epilepsy gives a kind of contact with the transcendent (readers of Dostoievsky will not be unfamiliar with this position). But the usual, and less heroic 'syllogism' would run as follows: prophets are epileptics; it is a bad thing to be an epileptic; so it is a bad

143

thing to be a prophet. Or more sophisticatedly: prophets are epileptics; epilepsy is a diseased condition whose causes are known; it is therefore likely that prophets have been deceived by the dramatic nature of their experiences into thinking them to be a sign of the active grace of God; but the grace of God does not work specially through diseases; so it is wise to assume that the prophetic claims are false. Though deflationary explanations trade on value judgements and are in principle compatible with joint explanations from the side of religion, their effect tends to be to undermine confidence in religious existence claims. This is because religious existence claims themselves are interwoven with pro- value judgements. Thus in late Victorian and Edwardian England, and in Europe, Freud's account of the genesis of religion, with its heavy sexual emphasis, was regarded by many of the orthodox as dangerously deflationary, because sexuality itself was somewhat disreputable, and so not valuationally compatible with the supposed ideals of Christianity. Things have changed somewhat since! The shocking character of Evolutionary Theory was also in part due to the low valuation of animals (apes especially), so that the derivation of man from the animals was deflationary. However, deflation is not the same as reduction. To true reductionism I now turn.

A truly reductionist account of phenomena of type X is one in which they are 'reduced' to phenomena of type Y. More linguistically: statements about Xs are 'reduced' to statements about Ys. In this sense behaviourism is reductionist. Thus Xs (mental states) are reduced to Ys (behavioural events, dispositions, etc.); or more linguistically, statements about minds are 'reduced' to statements about behaviour. Here I am thinking, for example, of Ryle's 'The Concept of Mind' (though it only went most of the behaviouristic way – thrills, tingles, and other mental occurrences stayed on, like appendices), a most ingenious and perceptive attempt to analyse mental statements as behavioural ones, chiefly through the use of a dispositional analysis. What might be called 'methodological behaviourism' in psychology may not be truly reductionist: it is just saying that the only thing that the methodological behaviourist concerns himself with is the overtly measurable, and so

144

methodologically neglects introspective reports. But still something more needs to be said: so far it appears that reductionism is a type of translation, or putting it ontologically a kind of identification. But the notion of reducing X to Y suggests that Y is more basic. But the main question, of course, is what is meant here by 'more basic'?

As it happens the Ryle case was mainly determined by epistemological considerations. Dispositions could be observed in their manifestations. This was a way in which the empiricist tradition of latter-day British philosophy is evident. Likewise it is not surprising that Skinnerian behaviourism is largely epistemological, or methodological if one prefers the term. However, the basic form of the 'basic' must be ontological. It is illustrated by certain cases of the hierarchical arrangement of the sciences. For example, among other things biochemistry involves a way of figuring out the structure of the genes and chromosomes, themselves vital to genetics, on a chemical basis. But in this context it could be said that the claims of chemistry represent something more 'basic' than those of genetics.

Unfortunately the attempt to produce a hierarchy of the sciences proves difficult. The reasons are various, and among them one can mention the following. First, one aspect of a given science may be ontologically prior (to use our jargon) to an aspect of another. An example has just been given above. But it does not at all follow that other aspects of what is counted as the same science are. Thus another part of biochemistry involves the processes involved in brewing, but this does not mean that the basis of brewing processes is ontologically prior to genetics. Second, what counts as a subject is to some extent socially, rather than logically, determined. For example, physics departments in universities do not usually concern themselves with astrophysics, and astrophysics is something counted in with astronomy and sometimes not. The determinants of subjects are often traditions and institutions intertwined, so that it is not possible to speak of a 'subject' as such (nowhere is the confusion more true than in the treatment of the elements falling under Religion in universities and colleges). So, second, the ontological argument of basicness falls under the threat of sloppy institutions and demarcational unclarity, not to say confusion. Third, the claim that one kind of event is somehow more basic than another (for instance that sensations are really brain states) can either proceed by identification or by a doctrine of levels. For instance, there is the philosophical idea of emergent properties, suggesting that a basic lower level spawns somehow a superior level of properties dependent on the lower level, but having a different set of characteristics. Maybe there are other options, but these have been the main contenders. As for the first, the argument must work both ways. For instance if sensations are brain states then brain states are sensations. In this context sensations are explanatory. That anyone should feel that this identity thesis threatens any view of the explanatory power of sensations is obviously ridiculous. Or it is ridiculous *unless* the identity thesis hooks up with the view that brain processes can be treated fruitfully physiologically, while sensations cannot be treated psychologically or however. In this case the brain processes take on a basic air, but the sensations and other conscious states persist. Do they play no role in explanation? If they do not, they have indeed a tension-inducing role. For by one token they are emergent properties, and by another they have no power.

Whether we proceed therefore by the route of identity or by the route of emergent properties there remains a problem about what counts as basic. Further, one should be on guard against the view that because X is *necessary* to Y it somehow consists in the essence of Y. Man is what he eats, or so it is said. But though eating is necessary to our social existence (and incidentally the converse is probably true, though contingently), it does not constitute the essence of listening to a lecture.

In brief, the whole question of the basicness of X to Y, in a complex and rich world, where the tools of analysis of it are various, complicated and partly determined by social and institutional considerations, is so confused that it would be unwise to assume *a priori* or even on the fragile evidence that a genuinely reductionist account of religion is possible.

By the same token it would be unwise to conclude that such an account is not feasible. To some extent the question is

146

metaphysical. But it would be as foolish to say that religion can be 'reduced' to whatever (say social psychology, though I put things very crudely) as to say that it cannot. Yet the question remains. It is to be answered by more investigation, just as the question of a physiological account of the psychological states of men is to be so determined. But the investigation is not just an empirical one. It is also importantly to do with the theory or metaphysics, the carving up of territory, lying behind it. We have already sufficient indicated philosophical, methodological, and institutional questions lurking behind the reductionist programme to make it plain that no simple approach to ontological basicness is possible.

This is evident in its way in the question of demonology in the New Testament. I have argued that the phenomenologist of religion and more widely the Religionist is unlikely to accept the 'theory' of demons evident in the New Testament. But why? The reasons in one way are not to do with the facts. We can easily accept that men and children froth at the mouth and that women go into cataleptic states. We can accept also that blind men can come to see, for there is hysterical blindness. But what we may accept as facts has to be fitted to a theory, or more broadly to a view of the universe. Thus the relation between reported facts and explanations is a subtle and difficult one. By consequence, the diagnosis of the 'true' state of affairs depends on many criteria. This being so, it is absurd to suppose that there is a single 'metaphysics' of the study of religion. What the Religionist accepts as plausible is bound to differ somewhat from generation to generation. It happens that institutionally and socially we live in a somewhat sceptical age. There are those who deny that folk are cured at Lourdes, though folk are cured there. There are folk who claim marvels for new sects, though the marvels perhaps do not occur.

In brief, if we look at the general question of a structural explanation of religious experience (the main theme in the present Chapter) the omens conflict. This is as it should be from the standpoint of the scientific study of religion.

Thus to go back a bit: the real power of an experience, such as Paul's, must be the subject of enquiry. It can be treated 'scientifically' even if the science of religion is different from

147

the natural sciences, for obvious reasons which have been spelled out previously. It is also true that the general reliability of a type of experience, from any Theological point-of-view, cannot be determined by Religion, though the philosophy of religion is highly relevant. And again it is surely true that general metaphysical arguments cannot as yet determine the basicness of one kind of 'reality' over another. That is they cannot show that religious experience is to be derived structurally from some other factor in human existence. But this is not at all to say that in the future things may not change. For so long as the scientific study, Religion, remains scientific it is capable of helping or hindering anyone.

Whatever may be thought about these previous discussions, it is clear that religion, considered phenomenologically, stays as a force in human affairs. So it is necessary to take its dynamic into account, just as one takes the march of science or music into account. If Religion has any edge over Theology (whether Christian or otherwise) it is because the Religionist attempts as far as possible to describe and explain religion, and so to contribute to the general stock of human knowledge and science. On the other hand the task of Theology is to Express a world-view and a commitment. If Religion has any share in this activity, it is at one remove. It cannot easily affirm, out of its own substance, that men are sinful or that the Creator is good. What it can do is to show that the understanding of religion, and even of ideology, is a necessary and indeed illuminating part of the human enterprise of accounting for the world in which we live.

Notes

INTRODUCTION

1. See my discussion with Bryan Magee in his 'Modern British Philosophy', pp. 166–77.

CHAPTER 1

1. See Jan de Vries' brief survey (cf. Bibliography); also the forthcoming '100 Years of Comparative Religion' by Eric Sharpe.

2. But see Lifton, 'Revolutionary Immortality' (cf. Bibliography).

3. Consider F. G. Healey's guide 'Preface to Christian Studies' (Bibliography).

4. See Bridget and Raymond Allchin, 'The Birth of Indian Civilization', pp. 311–12.

5. I here use an analysis of religion employed elsewhere, for example, in my 'The Religious Experience of Mankind', ch. 1, and in 'Secular Education and the Logic of Religion'.

6. Some of the discussion here is relevant to the thought of Troeltsch and others, but I prefer here to disengage the problem from the traditional and partly Theological discussion of 'the essence of Christianity'.

7. M. Eliade, 'The Quest', pp. 70–1.

8. C. J. Jung, 'Psychology and Religion', p. 117.

9. It is concerned with small-scale societies typically; but cf. the crack 'Sociology is about us; anthropology about them.'

10. John R. Hinnells (ed.), 'The Comparative Study of Religion in Education', pp. 22-3.

11. See Bibliography.

12. See my 'Doctrine and Argument in Indian Philosophy', pp. 214–16, and 'The Inapplicability of Western Terminology to Theravada Buddhism' in 'Religion', June 1972.

13. 'Reasons and Faiths', ch. 1.

14. See Bibliography.

15. See Zaehner, 'Mysticism Sacred and Profane' and 'Interpretation and Mystical Experience' in 'Religious Studies', vol. 1 no. 1.

16. 'The Yogi and the Devotee', p. 21 f.

17. This is not to say that the approaches in question cannot be fruitfully developed to cope with the new evidence. But the 'classical' theories of religion do run foul of important segments of the comparative evidence.

CHAPTER 2

1. See Bibliography.

2. The example refers to an actual case reported to me.

3. See 'Reasons and Faiths' ch. 1; also the discussion in D. T. Jenkins (ed.), 'The Scope of Theology', in my essay 'Theology and other Religions'.

4. Otherwise published as 'The Sacred Canopy'.

5. E. E. Evans-Pritchard, 'Theories of Primitive Religion', p. 47.

6. See, for example, Georges Dumézil, 'Archaic Roman Religion' (University of Chicago Press, 1970). For a general critique: C. Littleton Scott, 'The New Comparative Mythology'.

CHAPTER 3

1. For a general discussion of these and other issues see N. Smart, 'The Concept of Worship' (Macmillan, 1972).

2. To some extent this usage reflects an Indian one, namely that *devatā* can refer to both good and ill spirits.

3. Consider here the interesting and important treatment of parables in I. C. Crombie's articles in A. Flew and A. MacIntyre (eds.), 'New Essays in Philosophical Theology' and B. Mitchell (ed.), 'Faith and Logic'.

4. See my 'Towards a Systematic Future for Theology' in F. G. Healey (ed.), 'Prospect for Theology '(Nisbet, 1967).

5. For example, in M. Eliade, 'The Quest'.

6. To this extent Tillich's account of symbols could be justified; but there remain queries about how far my present account can be used in the metaphysical way suggested, for example, in Tillich, 'Biblical Realism and the Search for Ultimate Reality' – despite my astringent critique 'Being and the Bible', 'Review of Metaphysics' (June 1956).

7. Cf. 'Immortality and Life After Death' G. B. Caird and others, 'The Christian Hope'.

8. Cf. my 'The Work of the Buddha and the Work of Christ' in S. G. F. Brandon, 'The Saviour God'.

9. See the unpublished thesis by Ivan Strenski, 'Methodology and Myths with special reference to C. Lévi-Strauss and M. Eliade' (Birmingham University Library).

10 In Joseph M. Kitagawa and Charles H. Long (eds), 'Myths and Symbols', p. 135

11. See my 'Reasons and Faiths', ch. 3.

12. See Trevor Ling, 'Buddhism and the Mythology of Evil'.

13. Cf. 'Numen, nirvana and the definition of religion' in 'Church Quarterly Review, vol. CLX, 1959.

14. See I. T. Ramsey (ed.), 'Christian Ethics and Contemporary Philosophy' (S.C.M. Press, 1966).

15. G. Scholem in Joseph Kitagawa and Charles H. Long (eds), 'Myths and Symbols', pp. 175–6.

CHAPTER 4

1. See 'The perfect good' in the 'Australasian Journal of Philosophy.' (Dec. 1958).

2. Cf. p. 110. above.

3. See Bryan Wilson (ed.), 'Rationality'.

4. 'Reasons and Faiths', ch. 1.

5. D. C. Lau, 'Tao-te-Ching' (Penguin Classics, 1963).

6. E.g. ethical criteria could count. See my 'Reasons and Faiths', ch. 5

7. Philosophers and Religious Truth', ch. 3.

8. As in his 'The Secular Meaning of the Gospel'.

9. See J. M. E. McTaggart, 'Human Immortality and Pre-existence'.

10. Cf. R. S. Peters 'The Concept of Motivation' ch. 1.

Select Bibliography

The list of books is highly selective; in so far as the present volume is somewhat oblique to recent discussion in the philosophy of religion I have included some relevant nonphilosophical works.

INTRODUCTION

Ninian Smart, 'Reasons and Faiths' (London: Routledge & Kegan Paul, 1958).
——, 'Philosophers and Religious Truth' (London: S.C.M. Press, new edition, 1970).
——, 'The Philosophy of Religion' (New York: Random House, 1970).
——, 'Historical Selections in the Philosophy of Religion' (London: S.C.M. Press, 1962).
——, 'Doctrine and Argument in Indian Philosophy' (London: Allen & Unwin, 1964).
——, 'The Yogi and the Devotee' (London: Allen & Unwin, 1968).
——, 'Secular Education and the Logic of Religion' (London: Faber & Faber, 1968).
——, 'The Religious Experience of Mankind' (New York: Charles Scribner's Sons, 1969).
——, 'The Concept of Worship' (London: Macmillan, 1972).
Bryan Magee, 'Modern British Philosophy' (London: Secker & Warburg, 1971).

CHAPTER 1

Jan de Fries, 'The Study of Religion – a historical approach' (New York: Harcourt Brace Jovanovich, 1968).

Robert Jay Lifton, 'Revolutionary Immortality' (Harmondsworth: Penguin Books, 1969).

F. G. Healey (ed.), 'Preface to Christian Studies' (Lutterworth Press, 1971).

Bridget and Raymond Allchin ,'The Birth of Indian Civilization' (Harmondsworth: Penguin Books, 1968).

Mircea Eliade, 'The Quest: history and meaning in religion' (University of Chicago Press, 1969).

C. G. Jung, 'Psychology and Religion: West and East', tr. R. F. C. Hull (Yale University Press, 1938).

John R. Hinnels (ed.), 'The Comparative Study of Religion in Education' (Oriel Press, 1969).

Rudolph Otto, 'Mysticism East and West' (New York: Macmillan Co., 1928).

——, 'The Idea of the Holy', tr. J. W. Harvey (Oxford University Press, 1923, and many other editions).

R. C. Zaehner, 'Mysticism Sacred and Profane' (Oxford University Press, 1957).

Gerardus van der Leeuw, 'Religion in Essence and Manifestation' (New York: Harper & Row, 1963).

Charles J. Adams (ed.), 'A Reader's Guide to the Great Religions' (New York: The Free Press, 1965).

Milton Yinger, 'The Scientific Study of Religion' (London: Macmillan, 1970).

David Jenkins (ed.), 'The Scope of Theology' (New York: The World Publishing Co., 1965).

CHAPTER 2

Peter Berger, 'The Social Reality of Religion', otherwise published as 'The Sacred Canopy' (New York: Doubleday & Co., 1969).

Peter Berger and Thomas Luckmann, 'The Social Construction of Reality' (London: Allen Lane, The Penguin Press, 1967).

E. E. Evans-Pritchard, 'Theories of Primitive Religion'(Oxford: Clarendon Press, 1965).

Georges Dumézil, 'Archaic Roman Religion' (University of Chicago Press, 1970).

C. Littleton Scott, 'The New Comparative Mythology' (California University Press, 1966).

Herbert Spiegelberg, 'The Phenomenological Movement', 3 vols (New York: Hamanities Press, 2nd ed., 1969).

M. Merleau-Ponty, 'The Structure of Behaviour' (London: 1965).

Joachim Wach, 'The Comparative Study of Religions' (Columbia University Press, 1958).

——, 'Types of Religious Experience, Christian and Non-Christian' (University of Chicago Press, 1951).

CHAPTER 3

Ninian Smart, 'The Concept of Worship' (London: Macmillan, 1972).

A. G. N. Flew and A. MacIntyre (eds.), 'New Essays in Philosophical Theology' (London: S.C.M. Press, 1956).

Basil Mitchell (ed.), 'Faith and Logic' (London: Allen & Unwin, 1957).

F. G. Healey (ed.), 'Prospect for Theology' (Nisbet, 1966.)

Paul Tillich, 'Biblical Realism and the Search for Ultimate Reality' (University of Chicago Press, 1955).

Ninian Smart, 'Being and the Bible', 'Review of Metaphysics' vol. IX, no. 4, June 1956.

G. B. Caird and others, 'The Christian Hope' (London: S.P.C.K., 1970).

S. G. F. Brandon, 'The Saviour God' (Manchester University Press, 1963).

Joseph M. Kitagawa and Charles H. Long (eds), 'Myths and Symbols: studies in honor of Mircea Eliade' (University of Chicago Press, 1969).

T. O. Ling, 'Buddhism and the Mythology of Evil' (London: Allen & Unwin, 1963).

L. Lévy-Bruhl, 'How Natives Think' (New York: Washington Square Press, 1966).

C. Lévi-Strauss, 'Structural Anthropology' (London: Allen Lane, The Penguin Press, 1966).

E. Leach, 'Lévi-Strauss' (London: Collins, 1970).

Mircea Eliade, 'The Sacred and the Profane', tr. Willard R. Trask (New York: Harcourt Brace Jovanovich, 1968).

Michael Banton (ed.), 'Anthropological Approaches to the Study of Religion' (New York: Frederick A. Praeger, 1966).

CHAPTER 4

T. McPherson, 'Philosophy of Religion' (New York: Van Nostrand, 1965).

Bryan Wilson (ed.), 'Rationality' (Oxford: Blackwell, 1971).

Joan Brothers (ed.), 'Readings in the Sociology of Religion' (Oxford: Pergamon, 1967).

L. B. Brown, 'The Structure of religious belief' 'Journal for the Scientific Study of Religion', 5 (spring, 1966).

Gerhard Leuster, 'The Religious Factor' (New York: Doubleday & Co., 1961).

William A. Lessa and Evan Z. Vogt (eds.), 'Reader in Comparative Religion: an anthropological approach' (New York: Harper & Row, 2nd ed., 1965).

James H. Leuba, 'The Psychology of Religious Mysticism' (London: Routledge & Kegan Paul, 1929).

T. R. Miles, 'Religion and the Scientific Outlook' (London: Allen & Unwin, 1959).

W. P. Alston, 'Psychoanalytic Theory and Theistic Belief' in John Hick (ed.), 'Faith and the Philosophers' (Macmillan, 1964).

R. S. Lee, 'Freud and Christianity' (Harmondsworth: Penguin Books, 1967).

Anne Parsons, 'Belief, Magic and Anomie' (New York: The Free Press, 1969).

Index